create
SUCCESS!

create
SUCCESS!

←⋯ Unlocking the **Potential** of Urban Students ⋯→

Kadhir Rajagopal

ASCD • ALEXANDRIA, VIRGINIA USA

1703 N. Beauregard St. • Alexandria, VA 22311-1714 USA
Phone: 800-933-2723 or 703-578-9600 • Fax: 703-575-5400
Web site: www.ascd.org • E-mail: member@ascd.org
Author guidelines: www.ascd.org/write

Gene R. Carter, *Executive Director;* Judy Zimny, *Chief Program Development Officer;* Nancy Modrak, *Publisher;* Scott Willis, *Director, Book Acquisitions & Development;* Julie Houtz, *Director, Book Editing & Production;* Jamie Greene, *Editor;* Catherine Guyer, Greer Wymond, *Graphic Designers;* Mike Kalyan, *Production Manager;* Circle Graphics, *Typesetter;* Carmen Yuhas, *Production Specialist*

All Web links in this book are correct as of the publication date below but may have become inactive or otherwise modified since that time. If you notice a deactivated or changed link, please e-mail books@ascd.org with the words "Link Update" in the subject line. In your message, please specify the Web link, the book title, and the page number on which the link appears.

PAPERBACK ISBN: 978-1-4166-1113-4 ASCD product #111022   n3/11
Also available as an e-book (see Books in Print for the ISBNs).

Quantity discounts for the paperback edition only: 10–49 copies, 10%; 50+ copies, 15%; for 1,000 or more copies, call 800-933-2723, ext. 5634, or 703-575-5634. For desk copies: member@ascd.org.

Library of Congress Cataloging-in-Publication Data

Rajagopal, Kadhir, author.
  Create success! : unlocking the potential of urban students / KADHIR RAJAGOPAL.
    p. cm
  Includes bibliographical references.
  ISBN 978-1-4166-1113-4 (pbk. : alk. paper) 1. Effective teaching—United States. 2. Urban youth—Education—United States. 3. Students with social disabilities—Education—United States.   I. Title.
  LB1025.3.R355 2011
  371.1009173'2—dc22
                                                    2010044048

20 19 18 17 16 15 14 13 12 11   1 2 3 4 5 6 7 8 9 10 11 12

This book is dedicated to the memory of Dr. Lila Jacobs. As a professor, mentor, and friend, she inspired me to be an agent of change in urban education. She inspired me to get my doctorate and administrative credentials, and she connected me with other passionate educators in Sacramento State University's Urban Cohort. Regardless of where life will lead me, Lila's spirit will keep me committed to changing lives in urban schools.

create SUCCESS!

⟵ Unlocking the **Potential** of Urban Students ⟶

At a time when policymakers place so much emphasis on assessment, we finally have a book that addresses the two most critical issues affecting student achievement: effective teaching and student motivation. Several studies have pointed out that algebra is the gateway to college. Kadhir Rajagopal's important new book is an excellent guide that will show educators how to make algebra accessible and engaging to the students who most often experience failure in the subject and are prevented from entering higher level math and science courses. For those who realize that the pursuit of equity in education starts with providing effective teaching to all students, this book will be an invaluable resource.

—Pedro Noguera

PREFACE

Seven years ago, I entered the teaching profession because I wanted to help marginalized populations, especially urban and low-income youth. I am currently an algebra teacher at Grant Union High School, a comprehensive high school in a low-income area of Sacramento, California.

Algebra is often referred to as the gateway to college and high-wage jobs, but it is also known as the greatest trigger of high school dropouts. Over the past few years, my students at Grant have defied expectations and experienced success in algebra. In 2009, my students—who were all low-income and mostly African American and Latino—outscored the state average on the California Standards Test for algebra. They also outperformed the state averages for both Caucasian and high-income students. Therefore, they closed the achievement gap in terms of both race and income, which has been a perennial challenge for educators throughout the state and nation.

The model I developed, CREATE, is based on the strategies that I use in my classroom. This book presents that model, which has consistently led to success for low-income, urban students who perform below grade level. This book is intended to be a resource for all educators, especially teachers in grades 7–12 who are determined to unlock the potential within students who may have failed or struggled throughout their school careers and who may not always be intrinsically motivated to perform their best.

Many of the students whom I have taught in inner-city schools are brilliant and have as much potential as any student from a higher-income family that lives in a wealthier neighborhood. However, they may not accept their own ability to succeed in school, and they may have low expectations for themselves as learners. They may fear that exposing their academic intelligence will cause them to "sell out" or reject the "'hood" state of mind. They may act defiant and refuse any help, especially after years of failing and being told that school is not for them. As educators, we have a responsibility to expose the brilliance that exists within our students but has unfortunately been hidden after years of neglect.

For teachers of inner-city youth, the challenge of unlocking our students' potential is admittedly difficult, but it can be life changing. In this book, I refrain from making accusations or laying blame. Instead of pointing fingers, I share evidence-based strategies that validate existing practices and spark new ideas that can be used by any teacher—from any background—to engage urban students in learning. My plea is that you believe you have the power to effect change.

The single greatest factor influencing student achievement is the teacher. To help urban students, I believe that 90 percent of the battle lies within the will of the teacher. The CREATE model can help you transform that will into action. It will take patience. You might have to explain a concept more than once or in more than one way before students learn. Students' parents may not always cooperate, or their phone numbers may not work. In the end, you can't blame the students and give up because they are victims of circumstances beyond their control, internalized low expectations, and a system that has failed them year after year.

The CREATE model works for teachers who believe in their students and are willing to fight for them. Look inside yourself and consider: Are you one of those determined and passionate educators? Our students do not care how much we know until they know how much we care. We can—through love and stubborn will—convince our students that they are destined to succeed in school. We can help them become proud of being smart. Even more important, we can help them to actually experience success in school by developing positive relationships, setting high expectations, and adapting our instruction to their needs. We can empower them to unlock their potential.

Thanks for reading,

Dr. Kadhir Rajagopal

ACKNOWLEDGMENTS

I must acknowledge the support of Craig S. Murray, Darris Hinson, Wesley Marshall, Kim Davie, Wayne Hironaka, Virginia Avila, Jeanette Providence, Asad Akbar, and the rest of the Twin Rivers Unified School District family. Mr. Murray and Mr. Hinson brought me into Grant Union High School and gave me the opportunity to discover my talent and potential as an educator. I thank them for giving me the opportunity, recognition, and constructive criticism that I needed to develop into a dynamic educator for urban youth. Mr. Hironaka has been my mentor throughout my tenure as a teacher. He encouraged me to keep my head up despite the imperfections that exist within the urban educational system. His relationship with youth in the community also reinforced the importance of connecting with the heart before trying to connect with the head. Mr. Akbar is a great friend and human being who never hesitates to help others. He spent countless hours with me writing the first draft of this book and never asked for anything in return. It is rare to find such a giving human being.

Mr. Ram Ramanajum deserves a special thanks for his belief in me and my mission to change lives. He believed in me even when society questioned my intentions and my ability to make a difference as a teacher. I also have learned from Mr. Ramanajum that I must persevere in helping society but that I cannot save the entire world.

I acknowledge the friendship of Keith Hodges and Dr. Mary Gallet. Hodges inspired me to think big and pushed me to create a documentary and write a book that captured the success I was having with my students. Dr. Gallet introduced me to the world of speaking and sharing my success with educational stakeholders. She gave me my first opportunity to speak in public about my experience with youth. She also pushed me to contact ASCD and discuss with them the possibility of writing a book. I thank both of you for expanding my vision and helping me to find avenues for major transformational change in urban education.

Finally, I must express gratitude to my family—Thiru and Bhagu Raja, Amutha, Selvi, and Remya—for supporting me during my growth as a man, son, husband, and educational leader.

CREATE

An Instructional Model for Closing the
Achievement Gap in Urban Classrooms

Culturally Responsive Instruction

Rigorous Expectations and **R**ewards

Essentials-focused Planning

Assessing for Mastery During Class

Test Models

Extra One-on-One Tutoring for Struggling Students

INTRODUCTION: *The CREATE Model*

The student population at the heart of this book is composed of urban youth from impoverished neighborhoods, many of whom are African American or Latino. As a physical setting, these neighborhoods are usually characterized by poverty, liquor stores, gun shops, drug and alcohol use, and abandoned buildings that convey a sense of despair and hopelessness. In urban areas such as Oakland's Sobrante Park and Sacramento's Del Paso Heights, drug dealers, prostitutes, and gangs are an unfortunate part of daily life for far too many students. In this cesspool of negativity, however, many young people grow up among diligent working-class individuals and benefit from a strong sense of community and close ties with friends and family. Often, this environment provides a tight-knit community for kids because they know everyone from the local barber to the reverend in their church to the security guards at the ubiquitous liquor stores. This physical setting presents urban students with challenges and obstacles, while it also provides a sense of family and community.

Inner-city youth have to combat many negative influences such as pervasive substance abuse and gang rivalries, but the greatest obstacle that challenges urban students is often the "street mentality." This state of mind fosters much diverse behavior, but, most positively, it contributes to many kids learning how to be self-supportive—the so-called "survival instinct." Many of my students have been forced into the breadwinner role at home because their parents were in jail or simply absent. "Survival" for inner-city youth may mean working at the local store, selling drugs, or being physically or verbally intimidating so they don't appear soft or weak to their peers. Survival by any means necessary is a state of mind and a skill acquired by many young people growing up in these inner-city neighborhoods.

> "Children can't achieve unless we raise their expectations and turn off the television sets and eradicate the slander that says a black youth with a book is acting white."
> —PRESIDENT BARACK OBAMA

Unfortunately, growing up "on the street" often means growing up in an environment that leads young people, especially African American and Latino youth, to internalize the notion that they are not destined to succeed in school. Inner-city youth of color are often confronted by mixed messages. School administrators and teachers tell students that the path to success is paved with good grades. At the same time, various other influences in the neighborhood reinforce a mentality that glorifies individuals who acquire material wealth, lots of money, and respect through any means necessary—most notably sports, music, or drug dealing. This mentality (and, interestingly, the media) consistently reinforces the misguided belief that young, inner-city students of color should find nonacademic paths to success. As a result, many of these kids grow up to believe that doing well in school is "acting white," and an aversion to school subconsciously sets in and low expectations become internalized. Helping these students succeed in and enjoy school was the challenge that the CREATE model was designed to meet.

CHALLENGES OF URBAN COMPREHENSIVE SCHOOLS

Grant Union High School is a comprehensive urban high school. This means there is no selectivity during the student admission process. Inner-city high schools such as Grant tend to have a considerable number of English language learners (ELLs) or students with mild, moderate, or severe disabilities (including students labeled as "emotionally disturbed"). Indeed, almost 50 percent of Grant students receive special education or ELL services. Urban high schools also have many students who are far below grade level in one, more, or every subject.

At Grant, as at other comprehensive schools, we enroll any student who lives within certain defined boundaries. The students may enjoy school, or they may hate school. They may abhor and express their disapproval of every school rule. They may have

supportive parents or role models, or they may have no one to support them. They may have a history of coming to school once a month or a history of getting into fights. It doesn't matter. By law, we have to accept all of these students, and they become our responsibility.

Poor attitude, gang involvement, and a lack of motivation are serious problems that especially plague urban high schools. Comprehensive schools cannot easily expel students who break rules or miss weeks of class. If a student is younger than 16, it is very difficult to transfer him or her out, even if he or she has been the subject of interventions and continues to violate every truancy and behavioral rule. As a case in point, I have had students who show up to school once a month but are still left on the attendance sheet. Ultimately, their test scores (or lack thereof) will factor into and affect the teacher's and the school's overall performance.

There are many urban schools that produce amazing results, including 100 percent proficiency in math and science. These may be elementary schools where students do not come with the array of discipline problems that are characteristic of many urban high school students. However, it is more likely that these schools are charter schools or academies. Many successful schools, especially charter schools, can regulate who enters and leaves the school. The students may all come from low-income families, but those students chose that particular school and agreed to buy into its culture and expectations. They voluntarily do their homework, study for standardized tests, and comply with strict accountability measures. Students who choose to apply for charter schools are, generally speaking, more motivated.

Students who attend most charter schools also usually have parents who have made an extra effort to apply and attend certain meetings. By contrast, comprehensive school students don't have to be accompanied by a parent or make an extra effort in order to qualify for or stay in school. In fact, a student could enter and leave the school whenever he or she chooses. I have taken new students into my class as late as April without any basic algebra skills. Perhaps a student's family was homeless and just found transitional housing in the Del Paso Heights neighborhood; therefore, he or she is enrolled in Grant Union High School.

In addition, comprehensive schools cannot hire and fire teachers at will. There may be many great teachers, but there may also be several horrible teachers. When students have to suffer at the hands of bad teachers, it affects their overall performance in and attitude toward school. As a result of collective bargaining agreements, it is very difficult to get rid of a horrible teacher who is tenured. Meanwhile, a charter school usually has more power over the hiring and firing process. For all these reasons, the task of uplifting urban students in a comprehensive inner-city high school is very difficult.

Education is not all about testing and scores, of course. We are here to serve the students, even if it is difficult to really make a difference in their scores. We are here to affect and even save lives. We need to focus on the bigger picture and get *most* of our students to care about learning. Most kids will feel pride in their personal achievements and demonstrate their abilities on standardized tests once we instill them with the confidence and drive necessary to showcase their learning. Realistically, most students—even those in the "worst" inner-city schools—are savable with a great teaching force.

We must redefine success as more than just test scores. We must recognize and celebrate success when a student rises to grade level from far below basic. We must realize success when a student who was in a gang chooses to find a new sense of belonging in the marching band or community service club. I choose to be in a comprehensive school even though I know I would have an easier time improving student achievement and test scores in a low-income charter school. If we are not there for students in inner-city comprehensive schools, then who will be?

PRINCIPLES OF THE CREATE MODEL

In 2008, the special education students in my algebra class at Grant Union High School outperformed all students in the district. In 2009, my general education students outperformed the state average and went on to champion the notion that it is possible for poor students of any color—even though they may be far below grade level—to close the achievement gap in terms of race and income. The students were excited, and the district was shocked by the results.

The million-dollar question was why were these students outperforming their peers and succeeding in my class? To explain my students' success, I give credit to the CREATE model, which developed as the result of extensive interviews, student testimonials, personal reflections on my own teaching practices, and speaking engagements at the district, state, and national levels.

Several underlying themes are significant to this model. These themes, or fundamental principles, reach beyond the traditional teaching models used to address the needs of marginalized students who are typically left behind—too often our African American and Latino students. The model takes the traditional instructional strategies that are often taught in teaching-credential programs and asks the teacher to go the extra mile to reach marginalized populations. It also calls for the teacher to adapt the traditional teaching style to the needs of all urban students.

The CREATE model is grounded in three fundamental principles. The first is the belief that classroom teachers command the single greatest impact on student achievement (Marzano, Pickering, & Pollock, 2001). Quality instruction, therefore, is the most valuable weapon in the teacher's arsenal and the most significant factor that influences achievement gains—an influence many times greater than poverty or per-pupil expenditures (Sanders & Horn, 1994; Wright, Horn, & Sanders, 1997).

The second principle is the conviction that a teacher's race or gender has no bearing on his or her ability to foster success with urban students of color. In other words, a black teacher is not required for black students to succeed in school, and Latino students can learn from teachers who are not also Latino. With this in mind, it becomes apparent that the CREATE model is easily replicated—it can be used by any teacher in any classroom.

The final essential principle is the belief that all students should be held accountable for their success and that most students can be expected to succeed or show significant progress on standardized exams. Students can certainly demonstrate their knowledge and mastery of skills in numerous ways, including oral discussions, projects, and portfolios, but the reality is that students still need to be tested. Although standardized tests are often culturally biased, all students need to achieve success and pass those tests if they are to be competitive in society. Even though the accountability measures inherent in federal policies such as No Child Left Behind have their shortcomings, I believe they did force schools, teachers, and students to evaluate their successes based on student learning data.

> "We have given up on [students in urban communities]. We haven't given them access to quality education.... When we don't educate young people, we make them dangerous individuals."
> —STEVE PERRY

For most of my life, I have had an extreme dislike for standardized tests. When I was a student, I was easily confused by the wording of questions, and I experienced test anxiety. However, I would not be able to teach algebra or write this book if I hadn't learned to successfully take the SAT, the GRE, and the CSET for math teachers. Similarly, lawyers and doctors could not achieve their respective positions in society if they couldn't pass the LSAT or MCAT. The CREATE model, then, holds that teachers must expect urban students to remain accountable and meet a standard level of excellence—including standardized tests.

This does not mean that teachers should exclusively teach to the test and tell students when to circle *A* and when to circle *D,* for example. It *does* mean that teachers should be creative and incorporate real-life issues into the classroom, even if those issues are not explicitly discussed in the standards. It also means that teachers should teach standards-based content to mastery and prepare students to demonstrate their knowledge on a test accurately. In short, teachers should maintain accountability but not lose their ability to be creative.

ELEMENTS OF THE CREATE MODEL

CREATE is an instructional model designed to close the achievement gap in urban classrooms. The acronym represents the six components of the model:

C—Culturally Responsive Instruction
R—Rigorous Expectations and Rewards
E—Essentials-focused Planning
A—Assessing for Mastery During Class
T—Test Models
E—Extra One-on-One Tutoring for Struggling Students

The chapters that follow explain and explore each of these components in turn. When all six components are in place and working together, the CREATE model produces the desired results—it enables teachers in urban schools to close the achievement gap between their students and students from more advantaged backgrounds.

THE TARGET POPULATION

Although the CREATE model helps teachers reach all students, its primary mission is to empower teachers to reach those kids who are typically left out of or underserved in urban classrooms. These students form the base of CREATE's target population. In the United States, this population is disproportionately African American and Latino. Therefore, the CREATE model is meant to help educators specifically reach urban students of color.

"[A majority of low-achieving students] attend ... academically diverse classes in large, urban public schools attended predominantly by students in poverty."
—TOM LOVELESS

Within the target population, there are two types of students at risk for poor classroom performance. The first type is the student who struggles and acts out loudly. As a result of disengagement or a lack of understanding, these students talk when they are not supposed to, act out by throwing things, or repeatedly break class rules. The second type is the quiet or "under-the-radar" student who doesn't understand the material. These students won't tell you they are lost—they will quietly nod their heads and act as if they have mastered the content. They won't admit or tell anyone they don't get it. Unfortunately, their lack of learning will not be revealed until a test or major assessment.

TARGET POPULATIONS

Students who ...

- have historically been underserved in our classrooms.
- are primarily African American and Latino.
- are quiet and stay "under the radar" because they don't understand the material.
- struggle and tend to act out in class.

USING THE CREATE MODEL

The CREATE model can be used by any teacher in any subject. My own success using the model has been in mathematics. In California, the achievement gap is glaring in the area of mathematics. The failure in foundational math classes for urban students of color is evident in the fact that only between 8 and 10 percent of African American and Latino students are proficient in algebra, based on the 2008 California Standards Test (CST) of algebra. Overall, 65 percent of African American students and roughly 60 percent of Latino students who took algebra scored below the basic level on the CST in algebra. By contrast, 65 percent of white students and 80 percent of Asian students who took algebra scored at the basic level or above. This achievement gap is also seen in relation to income. In California, nearly 60 percent of students in low-income families scored below the basic level in algebra. By contrast, 62 percent of economically advantaged students scored above basic (Education Trust, 2008).

This statewide epidemic of urban math failure also adversely affects students in my own school. Grant Union High School in Sacramento has a 98 percent free-or-reduced lunch rate. It is a Program Improvement school (the formal designation for Title I–funded schools in California) with large numbers of underachieving African American, Latino, and Asian students. In 2009, the number of *F*s given in mathematics classes outnumbered all other grades. In the midst of consistent algebra failure, though, I have been able to achieve remarkably different results with urban students from low-income families. I have used specific strategies that helped most of my low-performing students succeed in algebra and perform at a basic or higher level of mastery. My students have consistently outperformed thousands of their peers throughout the district and state.

The success that Grant students have experienced with the CREATE model has been documented from 2007–2009, during which time I taught algebra to the Special Day Class and general population. The "special ed" population I taught in 2007 consisted of students with learning disabilities and behavioral challenges. A majority of the students were African American and Latino, and many came from single-parent or parentless households. Disabilities ranged from attention deficit disorder to mild cerebral palsy, and their math skills were generally at the 3rd grade level (according to traditional tests of basic skills and intelligence such as the Woodcock-Johnson test). Because of this, these students were not expected to do the same algebra or perform at the same level as the general population. However, I challenged them, and they defied all expectations by learning the same curriculum and taking the same standardized tests as their peers in general education classes.

In October 2007, the CREATE students in the Special Day Class took the districtwide midterm assessment and outperformed the entire district. My "special ed" kids had an average of 56 percent, and the district had an average of 46 percent. In December 2007, the Special Day Class took the first semester districtwide final exam. Their average score was 62 percent, while the district averaged 42 percent and Grant Union High School averaged 39 percent on that same exam. Furthermore, the Special Day Class outperformed the district—with an average score of 57 percent compared to 43 percent—on the third- and fourth-quarter algebra exams. It is important to recognize that the Special Day Class was required to show their work on each problem and not simply bubble in answers on the multiple-choice standardized exam. This effectively dispelled the notion that the students didn't understand the math or cut corners to arrive at their solutions.

In the Special Day Class, I personally experienced significant success with the CREATE instructional model. I also had similar experiences with the general population, which I taught during the 2008–2009 school year. Those students also performed at a higher proficiency level on every districtwide quarter exam than did their peers throughout the district. In April 2009, my CREATE students took the CST statewide algebra exam, and 71 percent of them scored at or above basic on the test, including 37 percent who scored proficient. In terms of percentage of students scoring above basic on the algebra CST, my students outperformed the rest of the school, the Twin Rivers Unified School District, and all of California (which had only 51 percent scoring at a basic level or above and 25 percent at a proficient level) (Gutierrez, 2010).

It is beneficial to note some revealing statistics that point to the power and success of the CREATE model. Specifically, 71 percent of African American students in my CREATE classes were at or above basic level, and 42 percent were proficient. For the state, 35 percent of African American students reached basic, and only 13 percent were proficient. Furthermore, 68 percent of CREATE Latino students reached basic or above, and 29 percent were proficient. This was higher than the state average for Latinos, which was 41 percent basic or above and 16 percent proficient. Interestingly, the state average for Caucasian students was 65 percent at or above basic level and 36 percent proficient. Therefore, both Latino and African American CREATE students outperformed white students statewide and effectively closed the achievement gap in terms of ethnicity.

Finally, CREATE students also closed the achievement gap in terms of income level. For low-income students in California, the average performance on the algebra CST was 42 percent basic or above, and only 17 percent met the proficient level. For economically advantaged students in the state, the average was 62 percent basic or above and 35 percent proficient. CREATE students at Grant Union High School had an average of 71 percent basic or above and 37 percent proficient. Therefore, the CREATE students exceeded the performance of similar low-income populations *and* economically advantaged students throughout the state.

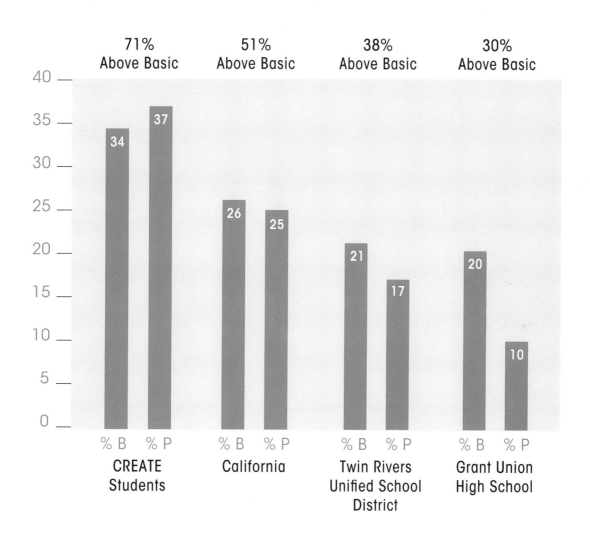

	71% Above Basic	51% Above Basic	38% Above Basic	30% Above Basic

CREATE Students: % B = 34, % P = 37

California: % B = 26, % P = 25

Twin Rivers Unified School District: % B = 21, % P = 17

Grant Union High School: % B = 20, % P = 10

B = BASIC

P = PROFICIENT/ADVANCED

RACIAL ACHIEVEMENT GAP IS CLOSED!

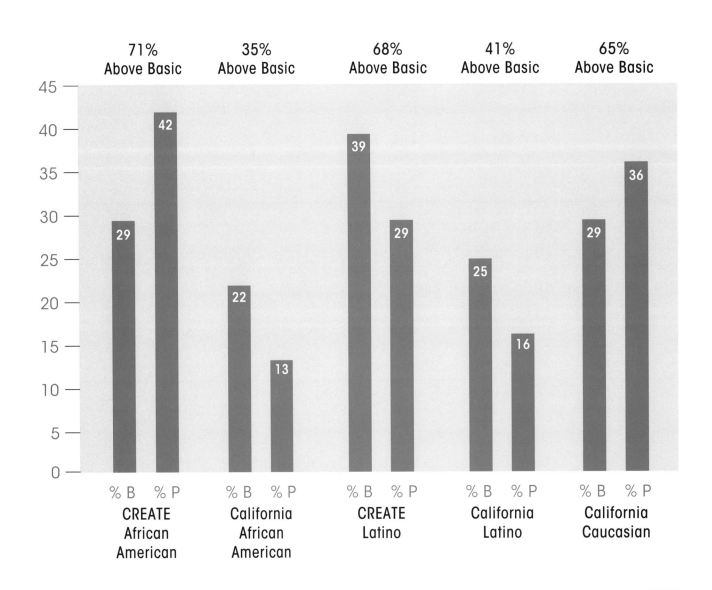

| 71% Above Basic | 35% Above Basic | 68% Above Basic | 41% Above Basic | 65% Above Basic |

| % B | % P | % B | % P | % B | % P | % B | % P | % B | % P |

| CREATE African American | California African American | CREATE Latino | California Latino | California Caucasian |

B = BASIC
P = PROFICIENT/ADVANCED

INCOME ACHIEVEMENT GAP IS CLOSED!

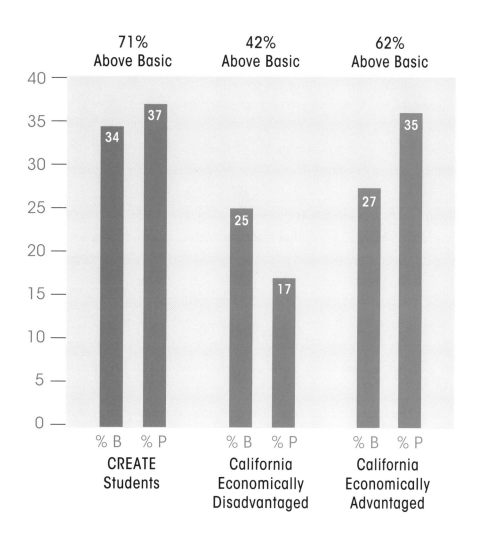

71%
Above Basic

42%
Above Basic

62%
Above Basic

% B % P
CREATE
Students

% B % P
California
Economically
Disadvantaged

% B % P
California
Economically
Advantaged

B = BASIC
P = PROFICIENT/ADVANCED

Comparisons within Grant Union High School were just as striking. Of the 87 students using the CREATE model in my four algebra classes, 33 students scored at the proficient level on the algebra CST and had an average score of 330. By contrast, of the 272 students in the remaining 13 algebra classes (that didn't employ the CREATE model), only 18 students scored at the proficient level and had an average score of 280.

In other words, my four algebra classes produced more proficient students than all other classes combined. When they first came to me, 80 percent of my students had scored below basic on the previous year's algebra CST. Not one of my students had scored at the proficient level, and most had received a *D* or *F* in their previous math class. Yet when they left my class, 71 percent of them had scored basic or above on the algebra CST, and 37 percent of them had scored at the proficient level. How was this possible?

By the end of the school year, the results that were coming out of my classes with the CREATE model had shocked the entire community and even aroused the interest of educators throughout the district. How could the Special Day Class, in particular, have done so well and outperformed thousands of other students in the district on every exam—exams they were not even supposed to take? How could the general population at Grant exceed the state average and close the achievement gap in terms of both ethnicity and income? Moreover, could the success seen in my classes with CREATE be replicable in other classrooms?

In the following chapters, I will explain how the CREATE model allowed me to achieve this startling success—and how it can help other teachers in urban school districts see similar results.

You may discover that you already use many of the CREATE strategies in your classes. You might find that you can improve on your existing practices with specific elements from the model. Furthermore, the CREATE model may inspire you to think of new approaches that will help your students learn. Keep in mind that the most important purpose of this model is to help *you* remain innovative and find what works best for *your* students.

A passionate teacher teaches as though his or her life depends on the student's outcome.

The underlying principle of CREATE is that high-quality instruction is the most significant factor for student success. Although this book attempts to present realistic, evidence-based instructional strategies, those strategies can never be a substitute for the will and energy of a determined teacher responsible for inner-city youth who have already failed and are not always motivated to learn. Educators who are not willing to take responsibility—and hold themselves accountable—for the learning that takes place within the four walls of their classrooms will not be able to take full advantage of this book or the CREATE model.

Truly effective teachers must be able to push disengaged or defiant students beyond their perceived limitations and fight until they realize success. They recognize that they must reach and influence their students' hearts before their heads. As a teacher at my school once said, "A passionate teacher teaches as though his or her life depends on the student's outcome." If you feel a stubborn determination to help your students, despite the resistance and obstacles you will encounter along the way, the CREATE model will help you to unlock the potential that exists within your students.

CHAPTER ONE: *Culturally Responsive Instruction*

The CREATE model asks teachers to provide culturally responsive instruction for their students. Culturally responsive (or relevant) teaching has been described as "a pedagogy that empowers students intellectually, socially, emotionally, and politically by using cultural referents to impart knowledge, skills, and attitudes" (Ladson-Billings, 1994, p. 382). What does this mean? It means that teachers make standards-based content and curricula accessible to students and teach in a way that students can understand. To do this, teachers must incorporate relatable aspects of students' daily lives into the curriculum. Such familiar aspects include language (which may include jargon or slang), prior knowledge, and extracurricular interests such as music and sports. Once students feel comfortable with how a teacher talks and discusses academic material, they will feel comfortable enough to focus and try to learn the content.

A common misconception about culturally responsive instruction is that teachers must teach the "Asian way" or the "black way." People often get intimidated by the words *culturally responsive* because of the incredible number of cultures and mixes of cultures in today's classrooms. Too often, teachers subscribe to the misguided idea that students of different races need to be taught differently, and they waste an enormous amount of effort in the process. Another result is that teachers usually appear fake by simply trying too hard to impress students of different backgrounds.

The key point here is that we don't need a different teaching method or curriculum for students based on race. I teach the entire class in a way that all of my students can relate to and understand, using aspects of their cultures with which I am comfortable. I don't want to stray too far from my comfort zone and consequently appear fake to the students I'm trying to engage. For example, I like to incorporate hip hop music into my lessons because many of my students relate to this style of music and I am also comfortable with it.

Hip hop is something my students (and many students) relate to and understand. You don't have to be African American, Latino, or from any particular cultural background to listen to a specific type of music or like a specific musician. When I teach complicated mathematical concepts, I tend to make analogies to cars, animals, sports, or other topics that will pique student interest. I try to capture their attention and find interests that are common to as many kids as possible. I don't teach by race. I teach to their collective culture. I find what appeals to most of my students—that I am also comfortable using—and then exploit these commonalities. Any teacher can do this. Any teacher of any race or gender has something in common with or can find something that relates to most of his or her students. Remember, though: Put it in their language, but don't come off as fake.

According to Crystal Kuykendall, a former executive director of the National Alliance of Black School Educators, "culture determines how children perceive life and their relationship to the world. Because culture also influences how and what children learn, educators can use culture to improve self-image and achievement. Not only must teachers show an appreciation of cultural diversity, they must also incorporate teaching strategies that are congruent with the learning styles of their students" (1989, pp. 32–33).

CULTURALLY RESPONSIVE RELATIONSHIPS

This has been repeatedly confirmed; if educators do not have some knowledge of their students' lives outside of paper-and-pencil work, and even outside of their classrooms, then they cannot accurately know their students' strengths and weaknesses (Delpit, 1995). This theme is also echoed by Pedro Noguera, who concludes that, in order to engage urban students, teachers must adapt their teaching to the way in which those students learn rather than the reverse (expecting students to

The **CREATE** model requires that teachers make a concerted effort to learn about their students' individual cultures and interests: language, sports, music, and so on. To achieve this, consider using surveys and question-naires, or build relationships by informally talking to students and asking about their interests.

adapt their learning to the way in which they are taught). Therefore, teachers need to know how to make ideas and knowledge meaningful to urban students and how to use students' culture and interests as tools to teach them (Noguera, 2003).

> "We must teach the way students learn, rather than expecting them to learn the way we teach."
>
> —PEDRO NOGUERA

During the first week of school, I begin building relationships with my students by using surveys and questionnaires to learn about some of their interests, I make time to talk with each of them, and I encourage them to share information about themselves. I have my students describe what a "good teacher" does in the classroom, and I then ask them to tell me what I can do to be the best teacher for them. Finally, I encourage them to share their negative experiences with previous math classes and give me ideas about how they would like to be taught.

As a result of talking to students and learning about their individual needs, I successfully convince them that I am an ally and willing to listen to them on their own level. This communication tends to make students feel hopeful because they recognize that their teacher is willing to adapt his or her teaching to their needs. I make an assertive effort to talk to students with a history of failure, behavioral challenges, or suspensions from other teachers' classrooms, as well as to students at risk for future failure.

> "We must keep in mind that education, at its best, hones and develops the knowledge and skills each student already possesses, while at the same time adding new knowledge and skills to that base."
>
> —LISA DELPIT

Early in the school year, I make sure to develop a connection with the most challenging students and gain a clear understanding of what may cause them to lose interest or emotional stability in the classroom. During the first few weeks, I strive to learn about all of my students, but I focus on the most challenging students so I can develop positive relationships with them and adapt the curriculum and my instruction to their way of learning. Usually, the most challenging students develop into the best leaders in my class—if I can engage them, I am usually able to engage the rest of the class.

CULTURALLY RESPONSIVE CURRICULUM

After teachers have gained an understanding of where students come from, they can incorporate learning styles, culture, background, prior knowledge, vocabulary, music, and sports into the curriculum. Keep in mind that the CREATE model does not ask teachers to *replace* the mandatory standards-based curriculum. Instead, it asks the teacher to *integrate* the traditional curriculum with material that is relevant to students' lives. Urban educators must question their teaching practices and develop culturally relevant teaching strategies to hook their students. To this end, teachers must use the cultural capital available in their classrooms to capture attentions, engage students, and make the academic curriculum relevant. The goal is for students to have increased access to the standards-based content they will need to take and pass district and national tests.

"Students must be … allowed the resource of the teacher's expert knowledge, while being helped to acknowledge their own 'expertness' as well."

—LISA DELPIT

In his book *The School and Society,* educational philosopher John Dewey argued that the development of curricula should be based on students' own interests (Dewey, 1889). Education, he felt, should be a child-centered process. Dewey believed strongly in connecting curriculum to the interests and activities of students. He felt that effective education required teachers to use students' interests to guide them toward an understanding of the sciences, history, and the arts. Dewey also urged teachers to connect each child's life experiences and interests to the existing curriculum. As a result, students would be able to understand and succeed in the traditional curriculum.

Dewey's philosophy has contemporary echoes as well. Robert Moses is a civil rights activist and founder of the Algebra Project, a national nonprofit organization dedicated to raising the academic performance of every child in America, a cause Moses describes as a modern-day civil right for minorities. One of the underlying principles of the Algebra Project is that "people talk" is used to relate math concepts to students. This principle implies that mathematical concepts in general, and algebra in particular, are discussed in language that is natural and intuitive for students before those students are exposed to the technical terms found in textbooks. Analysis of schools using the Algebra Project has shown improvement in test scores; supporters, however, point to the more important result: the perception that inner-city kids are neither interested nor proficient in math has been effectively shot down (Cobb & Moses, 2001).

In my own classroom, I am culturally responsive because I teach in a way that every student can understand. I use student-centered stories, vocabulary, and language. Student-centered stories and language are critical to hooking students' attention and making them receptive to learning the curriculum and textbook vocabulary. I constantly try to find ways to infuse hip hop, sports, and other student interests *without seeming fake.* It is important that you connect to your students, but it is even more important to be sincere and be yourself. Students have an innate ability to know when you're not being yourself.

For example, I use "street language" to explain the concept of isolating the variable in algebra. I say to students, "X is like a dog that wants his own block or neighborhood. Solving for X implies that it must be alone in its own neighborhood. X's neighborhood is separated from the other neighborhood by the equals sign, which acts as a gate. So

Student-centered vocabulary and language are keys to hooking students' attention and ensuring that they will be receptive enough to learn the curriculum and textbook vocabulary. Try to find ways to infuse hip hop, sports, and other student interests *without seeming fake*. Make honest connections, but be sincere and be yourself.

there are two different neighborhoods. Any number on X's block is like an enemy. In order for the number to leave X's block, it must change its operation when it crosses the equals sign (or gate). Therefore, if the problem is $X + 4 = 6$, then the positive 4 must leave the block and become a negative 4. $6 - 4$ is 2, so $X = 2$, and X is alone. The goal of solving for X is to get X (or the dog) alone."

Once students understand the story and the concept of isolating the X, I go back and teach the academic vocabulary. At this point, X becomes a *variable*. The students are more prepared and willing to learn because they already have a sense of confidence that comes from an increased level of comfort with the material.

Let's consider another example of culturally responsive teaching. English teachers can use a variety of methods to teach similes, including examples with familiar sports stars and relatable situations that involve similes and metaphors. For instance, "Kobe flies like an eagle to the basket, and the crowd is frozen in anticipation." It's also possible to use hip hop lyrics to teach literary elements, such as theme and tone. Many lyrics easily lend themselves to interesting and engaging lessons on mood or character analysis. Once the teacher hooks students' attention and makes sure they understand the relevant concept, he or she can then incorporate the standard textbook, which may include more traditional literature by Shakespeare, Faulkner, or Salinger. Students will likely be more willing to analyze a Shakespearean conflict if they already understand the concept from exposure to lessons that dealt with hip hop or stories that directly relate to their lives.

Within the confines of standard textbooks, teachers can often find multiple opportunities to connect a theme with their students' lives. For example, there are many Shakespearean themes—such as jealousy and greed—that students can easily relate to if the connection is made clear. The tension between the Montague and Capulet

(IN A CULTURALLY RESPONSIVE CLASSROOM)

$$X + 4 = 10$$
$$X\ (+\ 4) = 10\ (-\ 4)$$
$$X = 6$$

The left side of this equation is *X*'s neighborhood. *X* is the top dog in his 'hood and doesn't like anyone else on his turf. Solving for *X* implies that *X* must be alone in its own neighborhood. When a number leaves the *X* dog's block, it must change its operation. A positive number will become a negative number, for example.

CREATING SIMILES

(IN A CULTURALLY RESPONSIVE CLASSROOM)

The crowd fell silent and was **frozen in anticipation**. Kobe Bryant soared *like a bird* over the court. *Like an eagle*, he flew over LeBron James and dunked the ball. The basket **was a big nest**, and nothing could stop him.

families in *Romeo and Juliet* is similar to the tension that might arise if two lovers belonged to rival gangs or came from different cultures. Though it is an unfortunate situation, students in many urban settings can relate to the tensions that often lead to violence because of animosity between gang "families." Examples that build on experiences and situations such as this will usually get the attention of students in inner-city environments.

Relevant vocabulary will hook students' attention so they can eventually learn and understand academic vocabulary, the textbook, and the real world. Grab students' attention with their own language and stories before presenting academic language. Each population is different, though, and it would be a mistake for teachers to assume that *all* urban kids relate to gangs, basketball, or hip hop. The key here is that each teacher makes an effort to learn more about his or her students, puts himself or herself in their shoes, and figures out what it takes to make learning more accessible.

> Be creative! Teach in a way that relates familiar experiences to your students, and make the learning process as easy for them as possible. The textbook is just one resource (of many) you can use to achieve this end.

CULTURALLY RESPONSIVE DELIVERY

Another aspect of culturally responsive instruction that has been effective in urban schools concerns the delivery of instruction to students. Though it is critical to make the curriculum accessible and relevant to students, it is also important that the content be delivered in an engaging and interesting way. All too often, a teacher has a brilliant idea or lesson, but the delivery is so boring or didactic that students get turned off and miss out on the experience.

The CREATE model asks teachers in urban classrooms to make a focused effort at establishing an interactive dialogue with students, instead of delivering a one-way lecture.

Lectures often cause students to lose interest, and when their interest is lost, students are more prone to act disruptively. Effective teachers use a conversational approach and personally interact with many different students during the lecture portion of the class.

Research has shown that students typically retain the most information during the first 10 minutes of a lecture, so it is important to put limits on the amount of class time consumed by lectures. In fact, a traditional lecture may not improve student understanding at all, since it forces learners into passive roles. In order for learners to process and understand the relevant information, they need to be cast in more active roles within the classroom. Breaking the lecture into smaller chunks, and incorporating group discussions and activities into the curriculum, are ideal ways to accomplish this (League for Innovation in the Community College, 2006).

In urban settings, culturally responsive delivery of instruction requires continual interaction with students and frequent feedback. This highly interactive pedagogy can be conducted in a variety of ways, including question-and-answer techniques—the most powerful method I use to keep my students engaged and involved.

"Institutions that are culturally responsive and that systematically affirm, draw on, and use cultural formations of African Americans will produce *exceptional academic results* from African American students."

—THERESA PERRY

It has long been understood that questions are effective educational tools when asked before, during, and after a learning experience. The question-and-answer instructional style, then, has a significant impact on learning because questions are major vehicles for frequent interaction and academic feedback. One of the major factors that determine the extent of a positive effect and influence on students is the frequency with which teachers pose questions; the most effective teachers ask approximately three times as many questions. Dialogues that comprise question-and-answer exchanges allow for frequent academic interaction and provide numerous opportunities for students to be

If you lecture us for more than a minute straight, you'll lose us!

We need to be involved, please!

actively involved and receive immediate feedback. Students also feel an enhanced sense of self-esteem when they receive praise for positive input (Brophy & Good, 1986).

Academic discussions driven by question-and-answer exchanges also provide students with opportunities to receive immediate feedback they can use to control for mistakes, correct errors, develop as learners, and benefit from a more efficient learning process (Hannel, 2009). Questions must be specific and goal-oriented, and teachers must continually keep students focused on the established learning goals. Presenting too much information can cause cognitive overload or result in superficial

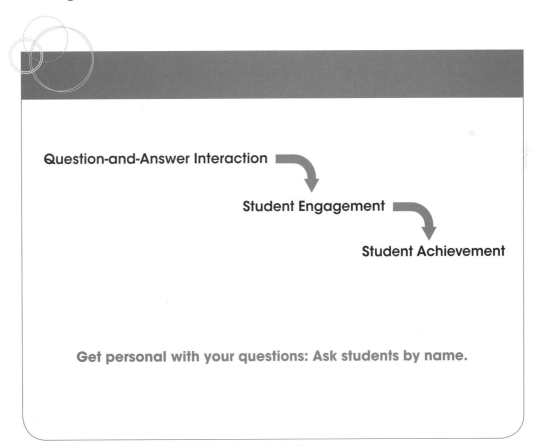

Question-and-Answer Interaction

Student Engagement

Student Achievement

Get personal with your questions: Ask students by name.

learning. A step-by-step lesson driven by questions and answers provides opportunities for elaborate feedback in digestible chunks that does not become overwhelming or ignored (Bransford, Brown, & Cocking, 1999).

These interactions are especially important for low-achieving students (or those with low self-efficacy) because they allow these students to improve learning and performance through a scaffolding process that encourages a step-by-step approach to problem-solving, allowing teachers to help students build from their existing skill levels (Graesser, McNamara, & VanLehn, 2005). For students new to or unfamiliar with a specific task, this process provides an avenue toward understanding while reducing potential frustration. High-achieving or more motivated students also benefit from the process by receiving feedback that challenges them, such as hints, cues, and prompts.

Create an interactive environment in your classroom with a continuing dialogue and conversation that runs at least two ways. Don't simply call on a few cream-of-the-crop kids whom you are confident will know the answer. Engage as many students as possible, especially the target population!

In the classroom, the CREATE model asks that teachers use questioning as a vehicle to keep students engaged during instruction. Make it a 30-way conversation, where you fire questions at all kids and everyone is in the "hot seat" and involved. In my classes, I ask a question every few seconds and have students teach back the step or concept I just covered. I do not wait for hands to go up voluntarily, and I try to keep everyone involved. By the end of a 15-minute lecture, I will have elicited at least 25 different responses, and I will have rewarded those students with points toward their grades (publically awarded on the whiteboard).

It is important that teachers use interaction that is more personal than general. I especially call on the target population (students who struggle and act out loudly and students who stay "under the radar") because I am aware that they will be the first ones to drift off or get lost. I avoid general questioning and instead call on individual students randomly. If only cream-of-the-crop kids are questioned or volunteer answers, teachers may mistakenly assume that everyone is listening. When a lesson favors students who are more attentive or already know the material, the target population can easily get lost, frustrated, or caught up in daydreaming. Unfortunately, these students won't reveal their confusion or boredom right away. Instead, those feelings will eventually manifest themselves as discipline issues or poor achievement on tests.

As I explain a concept or solve a problem in class, I make sure to ask three or four questions every step or two of the way. I also make a point to call on struggling students more frequently to ensure they are still engaged and following along. This interaction *must* occur logically and personally. For example, I might say, "John, tell me the next step in this problem." After John is done, I immediately call on another student to reiterate the same point or continue to the next step. I choose students to teach back to the class every concept I introduce and every step of a problem. I make every effort to interact with as many students as possible, but I focus my attention on the target population. Therefore, if I ask 10 questions, 7 will be directed toward students in the target population. If they can understand the material and stay engaged, then there is a good chance the rest of the class will also follow along.

In addition to question-and-answer techniques, I occasionally divide the class into teams and have them play math-related games. Playing games not only lightens the atmosphere, but it also helps students collaborate with one another. Even mildly competitive games encourage students to pay attention and be involved. There are many ways to conduct an interactive dialogue with students and keep them actively involved in the learning process. Remember that the key is to maintain an *interactive* lecture and to get personal with your questions.

Culturally Responsive

I N S T R U C T I O N

KEY POINTS

Relationships

1

---> **Learn** about your students' individual cultures.

---> **Adapt** your teaching to the way your students learn.

---> **Develop** a connection with the most challenging students.

Curriculum

2

---→ **Teach** in a way students can understand.

---→ **Use** student-centered stories, vocabulary, and examples.

---→ **Incorporate** relatable aspects of students' lives.

Delivery

3

---→ **Establish** an interactive dialogue to engage all students.

---→ **Stay** within your comfort zone and don't come off as "fake."

---→ **Continually interact** with students and provide frequent feedback.

---→ **Use** frequent questioning as a vehicle to keep students involved.

CHAPTER TWO: *Rigorous Expectations and Rewards*

Rigorous expectations can also be called high expectations. In sports, good coaches have definite goals for their teams. The coach of a basketball team may set a goal to make the playoffs. The same is true in business. The CEO of a particular company may decide that his or her business will increase its profits by 40 percent in the coming year. In these examples, the coach and the CEO establish themselves as leaders by setting realistic goals for their respective teams. Likewise, the CREATE model is based on the premise that the most important expectations begin with the teacher.

Teachers must have high expectations or goals for themselves, first and foremost, and those who produce the greatest academic gains must necessarily accept responsibility for teaching their students. These teachers believe that students are capable of learning and that they, their teachers, can teach them. Each teacher must assume responsibility for the fate of the students in his or her classroom; a teacher who truly is rigorous and passionate about getting results equates student failure with his or her own failure.

Research has indicated that the teacher is one of the greatest influences on student achievement (Marzano et al., 2001). Therefore, teachers must have high expectations for themselves and be motivated to meet those expectations. Research also shows that the efficacy of this process depends heavily on teachers' beliefs about their own effectiveness (National Center for Urban School Transformation, 2008). The National Center for Urban School Transformation (NCUST) is dedicated to identifying, studying, and promoting the best practices of America's highest-achieving urban schools in a manner that supports and transforms teaching and learning in all urban districts. NCUST emphasizes that teachers in high-performing urban schools must take responsibility for their students' learning.

If a concept has not been learned, then it has not been taught. This feeling of responsibility is echoed in the following analogy: A teacher who says, "I taught it, but they did not learn it," is like a physician who says, "I cured him, but he died"

(NCUST, 2008). In the classroom, I take personal responsibility for my students' achievement. If half of my students were to fail, I would feel like a doctor who has killed half of his patients. Therefore, if my students fail, I fail.

> "A teacher who says, 'I taught it, but they did not learn it,' is like a physician who says, 'I cured him, but he died.'"
> —NCUST

To create a rigorous culture of student buy-in and learning, teachers must be willing to do the following:

1. Set a high goal that you want your students to accomplish. Take responsibility for students' learning outcomes and be willing to adapt instruction to reach that goal.

2. Convey to students what their goals are. Instill in students the belief that they are on a mission to do something great.

3. Develop personal relationships and individual contracts with the most challenging students *and* their parents, coaches, and other supporters. Always follow through on the rewards and consequences stated in the contract.

4. Institute a reward system that allows you to provide immediate, visible feedback, and grade everything students do. Provide constant public recognition in the form of individual praise, bonus grade points, or tangible rewards.

SET PERSONAL GOALS FOR STUDENT SUCCESS

Passionate teachers in urban schools must exhibit (and encourage) excitement as they try to achieve important goals. In high-performing schools, teachers must create goals and get excited about accomplishing them. Teachers usually have objective and measurable goals for learning that pertain to students' progress or proficiency. Whatever goals are in place, though, they must be rigorous and push students to new pinnacles of academic success. For example, an English teacher may have a goal that all of his students will pass the high school exit exam. An algebra teacher sets a goal that at least 70 percent of her students will score above basic on the state algebra exam. A history teacher wants his students to outperform the state average on the state history exam. A science teacher strives to get her students to win first place in the state science fair.

When I was teaching algebra to Special Day Class students, I had a goal. I wanted my students to take the same assessments as the general education students and outperform them. No one, including my students, believed this goal to be possible. These students had learning disabilities, low skill levels, and a general history of failure. I made it a personal challenge to get these students to demonstrate learning at a level that was equivalent to, or higher than, the levels achieved by their "mainstream" student peers. As a result of being driven by a personal mission, I was able to help my students defy expectations and reach success.

CONFRONT STUDENT LEARNING DATA

Rigorous teachers consistently use accurate data to evaluate their progress toward student learning goals. These data can be derived from multiple sources, including standardized test scores, ongoing curriculum-based assessments, grades, teacher/parent observations and reports, and other anecdotal accounts of student development and learning. In far too many urban schools, teachers typically don't look at student learning data to evaluate their own effectiveness as teachers. This is because many teachers are reluctant to confront and reveal information about their weaknesses related to content knowledge.

In contrast, highly successful teachers are eager to confront these data. In high-performing urban schools, teachers generally feel comfortable admitting their own content-area weaknesses and seeking help to improve their pedagogy and increase student achievement (NCUST, 2008). CREATE teachers keep themselves accountable and feel responsible for student failure or success. They must be willing to disaggregate the data and analyze the performance of each subgroup of students. If it turns out that Latino students are doing poorly, for example, teachers must be able to see this in the data and think about possible solutions.

CREATE teachers, who have rigorous expectations for themselves and their students, are willing to address weaknesses or challenges that are revealed in student learning data. They are also willing to differentiate instruction and make whatever changes are necessary for improved student achievement. In short, they are not content until their students demonstrate mastery of essential concepts.

In typical urban schools, teachers present content and when they have finished presenting, they have finished teaching. By contrast, teachers in high-achieving urban schools are not finished teaching until they have collected evidence that students understand the content or are able to demonstrate the target skills. In my own classroom, I make it a daily habit to reflect on student learning outcomes. I assess students daily and, therefore, am in a position to evaluate my effectiveness based on learning outcomes. I often adapt my lesson plans or instructional approach to cater to my students' needs so their learning improves. I may change the seating chart in an effort to create an atmosphere that helps students focus and is more suitable to learning. I might "tighten up" my discipline and enforce detentions for students who persistently disrupt class. I try different styles of rewarding students to determine what will motivate them to buy in and become invested in the material. I am willing to do whatever it takes. Likewise, CREATE teachers must be willing to look at data and differentiate instruction in a way that improves student learning.

RIGOROUS EXPECTATIONS

Create a personal goal for student learning.
"I will get at least 70 percent of my students to reach basic or above on our standards assessment."

Confront student learning data.
"I got only 10 percent of my students to reach basic or above."

Take responsibility for student failure.
"Only 10 percent of my students reached basic or above. I have failed my students!"

Adapt your approach to help students reach the goal.
"I'll teach in a different way so at least 70 percent of my students will reach basic or above."

CREATE A RIGOROUS LEARNING ENVIRONMENT

"Expectations about a person can eventually lead that person to behave and achieve in ways that confirm those expectations."

—ROBERT TAUBER

In CREATE classrooms, students are presented with tangible goals. This happens orally, through banners, or through a mission statement at the beginning of the year. Then the teacher tries to convince students that they can and will accomplish those goals.

At the beginning of the school year, I tell my students that they will become the highest-performing math students in the district. I tell them that their goal is to outperform the state average on the state exams and disprove all the people who believe they cannot succeed. I inspire them by telling them repeatedly throughout the year that they will be the best and that they will be more powerful if they know math. Posters in the classroom reinforce the message that my students are #1. Students quickly begin to internalize this notion, and they begin telling their peers and parents that they are the best math students—a notion that is reinforced when they actually succeed on high-stakes exams. This aspect of the CREATE model is based on the veracity of the Pygmalion effect, which refers to the phenomenon in which certain students outperform their peers simply because they are expected to do so.

High-level and rigorous expectations for students necessitate a rigorous learning environment. Teachers with high expectations for themselves and their students create climates conducive to learning (Kafele, 2009). It is crucial that teachers in urban classrooms refuse to allow a few noncooperative students to disrupt their classmates who are motivated to succeed. The CREATE model subscribes to the principle that teachers have the right to determine what is best for their students and expect compliance. No student should prevent a teacher from teaching or prevent another student from learning.

> Fight for every kid, but never sacrifice the class for a few difficult kids. Consider the good of the many, and don't let any student prevent you from doing your job: teaching.

SEAT FOR SUCCESS

Another critical aspect of efficient learning environments that must be enforced, particularly in urban classrooms, is a mandatory seating chart. Teachers need to think about how to seat students, rearrange seating for easier access, and increase their proximity to students who are off task. A teacher's physical closeness to a student affects that student's time on task (Kiewra, 2009). Many of the "best" urban teachers use proximity to address discipline problems. If students cannot focus when seated

1. Give students challenging but attainable goals. Define your expectations for students.

2. Reinforce the notion that success is possible and expected. Maintain high expectations for students.

3. Encourage continual progress toward the goals. Help students develop high expectations for themselves.

> If we expect the best from our students, we will get the best. The Pygmalion effect creates a self-fulfilling prophecy where students rise to our expectations.

next to their friends, or if they are disruptive when surrounded by certain peers, it is critical to create and enforce a seating chart. CREATE teachers strategically seat target population students in a location that minimizes distractions (from friends and classmates) and maximizes engagement (with the teacher and material).

In my classes, I usually seat the target population in the front of the room and away from kids with whom they do not get along. I also modify the seating chart as needed. If a certain student gets too comfortable in a seat and starts to distract other kids, then I immediately "stop the bleeding" and find that student a different seat. If I did not enforce a mandatory seating plan, I would have to compete with students using cell phones under their desks, writing notes to one another, and having inappropriate conversations during class.

I have seen many classrooms without a seating chart, and half of the students are not engaged with the class material because they are already far too engaged with their best friends, whom they are sitting beside. I have also witnessed many teachers who create seating charts but don't aggressively enforce them. Instead, they let students sit wherever they want after the students complain and make a little noise.

> "Interaction between teachers and students is the most important factor in student motivation and involvement."
> —RICHARD TIBERIUS & JANE TIPPING

Once students see that a teacher is soft or lax in enforcing rules, they will try to "punk" or take advantage of that teacher. During my first year of teaching, this unfortunately happened to me all the time. Being a young teacher, I had to constantly remind students that I was not their friend and that I was in charge. Once I was able to demonstrate my authority (and commitment to their success) by seating students where they could focus, I began to experience success with my students, and the classroom environment quickly went from dysfunctional to functional.

Sure, many of my students continue to retaliate and complain. They don't like the fact that I am the only teacher who actually enforces a seating chart. They are used to teachers who talk about the seating chart but rarely enforce it. Ultimately, I don't care if my students like me. I don't care if I am not their favorite teacher. I *do* care about their learning and progress. I know that my students are able to learn when they are in a setting where they can focus. If I have a student's attention—and I don't have to compete with irrelevant distractions—then I can capitalize on the opportunity to engage that student in learning, and I am usually able to maintain his or her attention until the instruction is over.

DEVELOP A RELATIONSHIP OF TRUST

When it comes to discipline and student engagement, I firmly believe that good instruction will solve most problems in urban classrooms. Instruction that is dynamic and interactive will engage most students, who will not then behave poorly as a result. If students are not following class rules, look to the quality and delivery of instruction before anything else. In most inner-city classrooms I have observed, the key reason students are not engaged is because the instruction is not engaging. It is too often the case that teachers deliver one-way lectures and never interact with students on a personal level.

In some classrooms, though, a few students do not comply with the rules even when they are provided with the best possible instruction. In each of my classes, I have had to struggle with four or five students who do not readily comply with rules, despite powerful instruction. If allowed, these students can set the tone for the class and dictate their classmates' behavior. They can ruin the whole class—or lead the class in a positive direction with proper motivation.

Don't allow

- A few difficult students to run your class.
- Students to sit with their friends.
- Talking, especially while you are teaching.
- Sleeping during class time.
- Students to sit where they will be distracted.

Develop a positive relationship
with challenging students.
Be a mentor!

Teachers in urban classrooms need to devote extra effort to developing relationships that are based on trust and accountability. A relationship of mutual trust with the most challenging students can be what saves an entire class. If I have a student who constantly breaks the rules or cuts class, I make it a point to have a one-on-one conversation with that student. I make time during lunch or after school and create "space" for the student to tell me his or her side of the story completely.

The level of personalization in a classroom has been shown to be directly related to students' academic achievement (McClure, Yonezawa, & Jones, 2010). In this context, *personalization* refers to the existence (and quality) of connections among students, teachers, administrators, and other adults at school. Students who act out or are disengaged may be dealing with personal issues that are not readily apparent within a classroom setting. For example, I have had students who were homeless or experienced the death of a parent. The frustration that results from such situations can often inappropriately manifest itself in the classroom. Therefore, I talk to my most challenging students (or to their parents/guardians) on an individual basis to determine what issues might be affecting them. I talk to them in a firm but uplifting way that will, I hope, motivate them to improve. It is crucial to approach students in a positive manner. I try hard to convince my students that I am an ally and on their side, even when they make mistakes. Usually, the personal attention I give them during these conversations helps my students improve their own behavior. When they see that their teacher really cares, they often comply and work for the teacher. In addition, I may call a student's parent(s) to learn about the situation and express that I am ready to help the student in any way possible. To help the most difficult students reform their own bad behavior, it is often more effective to enlist the aid of a parent or coach—sometimes the most significant person in a student's life— than to involve the school principal.

CREATE INDIVIDUALIZED CONTRACTS

There are, of course, a few students who simply won't comply, despite my best efforts to show compassion and enlist the aid of parents or coaches. For those students, the issue might be that they require "tough love" or accountability. I therefore work with them to develop contracts that help keep them accountable for their own improvement. These contracts are agreements that the student and teacher must sign and promise to honor. They lay out the solution or corrective action the student will take to fix the problem at hand, as well as the consequences that will happen if the student fails to honor his or her word.

If the issue is persistent tardiness to class, for example, the contract will clearly state that the student *must* arrive on time. If the student does not comply with this, there *will* be consequences, including lunch detention with the teacher or phone calls to the parents or athletic coach. I have kept students after school for breaking their contracts, and, as a result, they missed football or basketball practice. For many students, this is a more-than-adequate motivator. It is important that these consequences are not empty threats; teachers must also honor the contract and follow through with any necessary repercussions. Once students see that the teacher is "not playin'," they usually comply with their contractual agreements.

My cell phone has been my best friend. My students know that if they do not comply with their contracts, I will be on the phone with the basketball coach, an older sister, or a parent, for example. On several occasions, I have had coaches give a speech in class to help their players focus. When students understand the reality of the situation—that their parents or guardians will stay in the picture to keep them accountable—they begin to appreciate the role I play. When they see that I actually enforce the consequences included in the contracts, they are quick to comply and respect my authority.

My students know that I do not make idle threats. The worst possible action a teacher could take is a failure to enforce a contract's consequences. This negligence not only convinces students that the teacher isn't serious about the process but also undermines the teacher's authority. It may take some time before a student starts to comply with expectations, but accountability is key. Students must see that their teacher means everything he or she includes in the contract. The individualized nature of the relationship or contract that is formed with the most challenging students is significant—it has saved most of my students who could have been behavioral challenges.

By developing relationships based on trust and accountability, I can reach at least 80 percent of my students every year. Nevertheless, there are always a handful of students whom I cannot reach, no matter what. If I have exhausted all of my power and energy in helping a student and still fail to help him or her turn the corner, I have to start thinking about damage control. I simply cannot sacrifice a class of 25 students in order to save one or two. For those few students who don't come to class or comply with the rules, I aggressively seek support from the school counselor or administration to set up intervention meetings. In extremely rare situations, the most appropriate action might be to keep the disruptive student out of the classroom, through suspension or a schedule change, in order to better serve the rest of the class. Even though powerful instruction and positive relationships are the keys to reaching a vast majority of students, it is not possible to win every battle.

USE REWARDS TO PROMOTE STUDENT MOTIVATION

Interest and motivation are essential elements in the learning process. No one—young children, high school students, or adults—will learn until they are both ready and sufficiently motivated. Therefore, it is critical to get students to buy in and participate in the learning process. Once again, the quality of instruction is the most significant factor in student engagement, but motivation may also come as a result of extrinsic incentives. It may seem obvious that students are more inclined to learn about topics that interest them personally, but their motivation to continue learning is also influenced by what they perceive as their ability to succeed or fail (Slavin, 1995). Therefore, if instruction is powerful and makes the material appear rigorous but still attainable, students will likely buy in and be motivated to try. If the material appears foreign or too difficult, students are less likely to give their best effort. Student buy-in is high when the level of instruction is appropriate and when they perceive material can be mastered with effort—making the payoff valuable and rewarding.

"African American students will achieve in school environments . . . where the expectation that everyone achieve is explicit and is regularly communicated in public and group settings."

—THERESA PERRY

Clearly, it is impossible to reach every student with every topic. When the intrinsic interest value of a lesson fails to engage students, incentives such as public praise and extra-credit points often help bridge the gap and motivate students. Positive reinforcement motivates students to do what is right and to continue doing what is right. Urban schools that produce high-achieving students engage in public demonstrations that communicate and celebrate high achievement. Small and large successes are celebrated often (NCUST, 2008). Rewards that are frequent, public, and personal can help raise the achievement of urban students. Tangible rewards— such as prizes, food, and certificates—are examples of positive reinforcement that encourages "rewardable" behavior to recur in the future.

In my classroom, I use many different forms of positive reinforcement to get students to buy in and focus on the material. The greatest (and most frequent) reward I provide students is immediate feedback on or points for their work in class. The power of an immediate grade is significant. Students are like most people; they want to be compensated for their work. Therefore, I reward everything they do. The warm-up activity and lecture notes are worth 20 points, and the independent assignment is worth 30 points. Every day, students have the opportunity to get "paid" 50 points if they have successfully completed their work. There is little ambiguity to this compensation since students know exactly how many points are at stake if they fail to do their work in class.

> Value each student's contribution to class. Make students feel like they are getting "paid" for everything they do (participation, assignments, exit price, etc.). Make it cool to learn and succeed.

Students typically work harder when they know where the road will lead them and when they recognize what's at stake if they successfully follow the road to its end. This is why a concrete grade is one of the most powerful motivators, but it must be delivered with immediacy and as compensation for students' efforts. Immediate feedback has been shown to increase student achievement by 37 percent (Marzano et al., 2001). Students must feel that there is value to everything they do in the classroom, and they should be continually aware of the grade or compensation they earn from doing their job in class.

Use a public scoring system

Every class starts with a scoreboard that includes the names of all students in that period. I use small, portable whiteboards that are easily displayed but are still visible to all students. It's a good idea to have separate scorecards for each class, so you only need to write the students' names once, at the beginning of the year. This saves a lot of effort on your part and a lot of class time. You do not *need* to use whiteboards for this, though—preprinted sheets of paper work equally well.

All students get "paid" for the work they do daily. I usually calculate this work to be worth 50 points toward their grade. Therefore, each student begins each class with

Rewards →

Student Engagement →

Student Achievement →

Culture of Learning

50 points beside his or her name on the scoreboard. This is significant because each student sees that he or she will get paid 50 points upon successfully completing the day's assignment and exit price. The key word here is *see*. Rewards have to be tangible or visible. When students see the 50 points beside their names on the scorecard, they are constantly reminded of the reward they are working for. That is a tangible incentive for students to work hard.

Offer bonus points for class participation

In order to get bonuses or gain extra points, students must contribute to a group discussion or to the overall learning of the class. When I call on students to do a certain part of a problem, I immediately reward them with an extra five points. I add these points to their original 50 on the scorecard. A student can get paid an additional five points for answering each question that I ask him or her or for volunteering an answer by raising his or her hand. I fire many questions at many students, especially the target population, so that class is interactive and I can assess if students understand what I am teaching. When I get the most challenging students involved, the culture of the class is set, and it becomes "cool" to get bonus points on the scoreboard.

> When the most challenging students are involved, the culture of the class is set, and it becomes "cool" to get bonus points and succeed.

As I have mentioned, the most challenging students often become the leaders of the class, and their actions influence what other students do and accept. Even if students respond incorrectly, I still reward them for trying. Remember, students want to know that what they say or do is valued. Therefore, I acknowledge every positive thing that students do. Though I do call on students who raise their hands, I do not wait for volunteers. I usually choose kids randomly and ask them to teach back a certain step in a math problem. This eventually places every student in the hot seat and even "under-the-radar" students can be rewarded publicly. The main idea is that students get paid for every response, whether elicited by me or volunteered, and they see their rewards on the scoreboard. I also reward points for good citizenship or acts of kindness. If a student helps another student in a significant way with the class work, then I may give 10 extra points. I make it cool to be a great student *and* person.

The reward process for participation should not be general. Individual students, especially those in the target population, must feel rewarded or recognized. Teachers must not simply say, "Great job, class." Instead, teachers should individually acknowledge students in front of everyone and reward them with points toward their grade. For example, "Antoine, you get five bonus points for doing the next step in solving the problem" or "Tina, I'll give you 10 bonus points if you can do this problem on the board." I constantly reward individual success publicly. Every response in class is rewarded with points on the board. This makes success visible and personal.

Enforce penalties on the scoreboard

Of course, students can lose points too. The biggest way to lose points is to not complete the class assignment or exit price. If students don't successfully complete the daily task (or impress me with effort), then they will see their 50 points on the scoreboard turn into a 0. It is important that they *see* this happen in class. Toward the end of each class, I go to the scoreboard and turn the 50 into a 0 for those students who fail to complete the assignment. In addition, when those students check their grades online or on a progress report, they will see a 0 instead of a 50 for the particular assignment.

I also make it clear that there are six behavioral violations that can cause students to lose points or get fined. Make your list public so there is no ambiguity, but be fair to all students. Avoid the danger of playing favorites and only penalizing certain students. I give students ample warning before I take away points, and I use my best

TOTAL POINTS

Montray: 50 + 5 + 5	60
Darlesha: 50	50
Tina: 50 + 5	55
Antoine: 50 + 5 + 5	60
Tony: 50 + 5	55

This sample scoreboard shows the initial 50 points each student begins class with, plus bonuses earned for correct responses. Since Antoine participated twice and did his assignment in class, he will receive 60 points out of 50. Hence, he got an *A+* for the day, and he knows it when he leaves class.

VIOLATIONS

Failure to

- Pay attention during lecture (no phones, iPods, talking, etc.) – 20 pts
- Use positive language (no curse words, derogatory names, etc.) – 20 pts
- Be on time – 10 pts
- Respect your peers or teacher – 20 pts
- Sit in your assigned seat – 20 pts
- Get permission before leaving class – 20 pts

judgment to decide when to subtract points and how to be fair. My goal is to improve behavior and learning—not to punish students or battle with them over points.

Offer tangible rewards when necessary

Not every student will respond to the 50 assignment points or to potential bonus points. I have found that giving tangible rewards, such as candy, is another useful way to engage students. I have various types of candy that students can buy using their bonus points, and I value each one at 10 points. Students must decide if they want to keep their bonus points or satisfy a sweet tooth. If a student has earned an additional 30 bonus points during class, for example, he or she has the opportunity to buy up to three candies with those points. After the student buys the candy, I erase the appropriate number of points from the scoreboard. In my experience, fewer than 10 students in a class choose to spend their bonus points on tangible rewards. In other words, most students recognize the value of additional bonus points toward their grade.

It's not necessary to spend a lot of money on these rewards. I usually go to the dollar store and spend a nominal amount each week. I have also received donations that I used as a fund to buy rewards—primarily from various dollar stores, national big-box stores, and supermarkets. Remember, it is *not necessary* to use treats to get students to buy in. Simply, rewards for completing an assignment and bonus points for extra work or participation can get *most* students to try hard, and I have found that *some* students respond even more when I use tangible rewards. The critical point here is that students appreciate and respond to immediate tangible or visible rewards for their work and want to be kept accountable for what they do.

Record total points for each student

Students want to see that they are really paid for their work. Therefore, I record each day's total points, and students can then see their grades online or on the progress report. They can also see that their bonuses were factored in, and this reinforces for them that hard work is rewarded. It is critical that students also see their penalties and that they are actually held accountable for them. This also reinforces the fact that you, the teacher, are serious about keeping them accountable. Once this becomes routine, the culture of the class will head toward positive behavior and achievement. If students see that they aren't rewarded for their work or aren't punished for violations, then they will internalize the notion that the teacher doesn't keep his or her word. They may stop working hard (or at all) because they simply don't trust their teacher.

I record each day's points during lunch, prep period, or after school. It takes about five minutes for each class. Many schools have convenient computer programs that standardize the grading process. For example, I can input each student's grade to the school computer system, and students or parents can then access the grades online. This is yet another way to share students' successes and make their rewards public. Accountability is critical; it helps show students that every action they take *matters*.

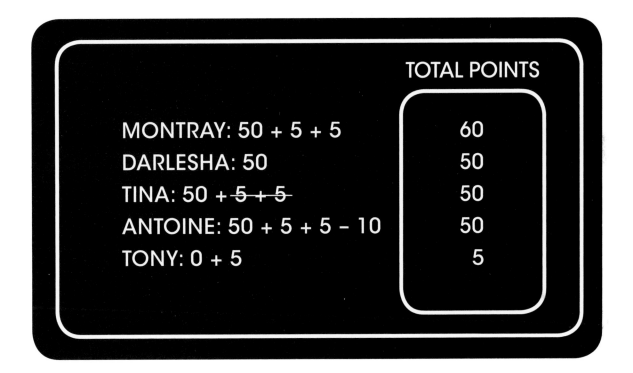

TOTAL POINTS

MONTRAY: 50 + 5 + 5   60
DARLESHA: 50   50
TINA: 50 + 5 + 5   50
ANTOINE: 50 + 5 + 5 – 10   50
TONY: 0 + 5   5

Here is a typical scoreboard at the end of a class, which accounts for assignment points, bonus points, and penalties. The penalties are usually few because, after a few weeks, students buy into the system and want to keep their points and gain bonus points. For this class, Tina used 10 points to buy a tangible reward; Antoine was penalized 10 points—most likely as a result of poor behavior; and Tony did not do his assignment (or impress me with his effort), so he didn't earn any points for the assignment.

Rigorous Expectations

A N D   R E W A R D S

KEY POINTS

1 RIGOROUS EXPECTATIONS
for Teachers

---> **Take personal responsibility**
for your students' success.

---> **Use assessment data** to evaluate
your own teaching effectiveness.

---> **Differentiate instruction** to raise
student achievement.

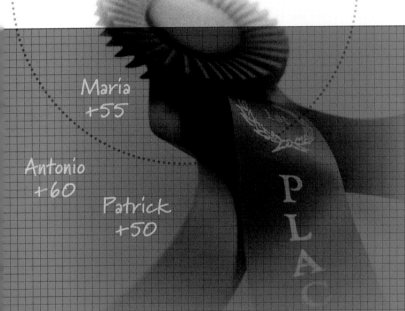

Maria +55

Antonio +60

Patrick +50

3 REWARDING
Expectations

⟶ **Create** a class culture that rewards student learning.

⟶ **Foster** a culture of positive feedback.

⟶ **Enforce** penalties and consequences, when necessary.

⟶ **Reward** student success, no matter how small.

2 RIGOROUS EXPECTATIONS
for Students

⟶ **Help** students establish and internalize measurable goals.

⟶ **Create** a positive learning environment with few distractions.

⟶ **Promote** a relationship of trust.

⟶ **Develop** individual learning contracts with challenging students.

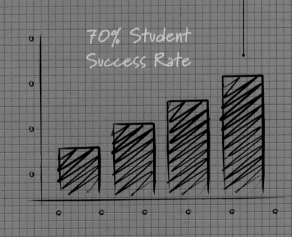

70% Student Success Rate

CHAPTER THREE: *Essentials-focused Planning*

The next aspect of the CREATE model is that teachers focus on and plan for mastery of essential concepts. According to the National Center for Urban School Transformation (NCUST), an organization that studies the most successful urban schools in the United States, teachers in high-achieving urban schools do not teach or assess *everything*. Rather, they teach and assess the *most important* things exceptionally well (NCUST, 2008).

Teachers should target and exclusively focus on students' mastery of essential concepts rather than attempt to teach every concept to the possible detriment of student learning. In traditional urban schools, the textbook is the curriculum. Usually, curriculum-alignment processes have generated pacing charts designed to ensure that all standards are covered well. In contrast, NCUST shows that high-performing Title I schools teach fewer objectives in greater depth. Educators in these schools tend to identify critical standards and then focus their attention on teaching them well (NCUST, 2008).

"Increased student learning [is] the only objective measure of a teacher's success."

—MICHAEL B. POLIAKOFF

Mastering a skill requires a fair amount of focused practice, and it is important to restate essential principles frequently. Urban schools that demonstrate measurable improvements in student success typically establish objective methods to determine whether their students have gained a level of proficiency that places them on par with the state assessment. By ensuring that students learn critical standards well, educators reduce the amount of "drive-by teaching," which, according to NCUST, occurs when teachers feel rushed to cover every concept in the textbook and are unable to ensure comprehension. As a result, students might learn very little, or they may gain only a superficial understanding of a few concepts.

INSTRUCTION MUST REFLECT STUDENTS' NEEDS

To get students to master the essential concepts, teachers must first take several important steps. Begin by creating a pacing guide for instruction that is based on how long it will take students to master essential concepts. (Most teachers will know how much time students require to master concepts from past experience. In addition, diagnostic assessment data should give a rough idea of most students' skill levels and indicate the amount of scaffolding necessary to master a concept.) For example, I create a pacing guide during the summer that is based on the essential standards blueprint for my state. For Algebra I, the state blueprint lists about 15 key standards. Some of these standards are related and can be grouped together, so there may be only 10 distinct standards. From this, I create a timeline based on key concepts that helps me pace my instruction.

It is important to note that CREATE teachers do not "live or die" by the district or textbook pacing guides when they plan instruction. These guides make good resources, but they should not be used as inflexible rules for instruction. In reality, they may not accurately reflect students' individual learning needs, so teachers must plan instruction for the year based on their own students' specific learning needs.

Make your own pacing guide that is tailored to the specific needs of individual students. District and textbook pacing guides are resources that lay a foundation from which an individualized pace can be set. Students' needs should drive the real pacing guide.

As I create a timeline for instruction, I take into account how long it will take my students to master concepts. The key words here, obviously, are *my students*. My students are different from many of the students whom textbooks are designed to teach. Textbook pacing guides usually assume that students are at grade level. If an average student who is at grade level needs a week to learn a particular skill, then most textbooks make the blanket assumption that all students will learn that skill within a week and teachers can then move on to the next concept. However, my students—and a majority of students in inner-city math classrooms—are several levels behind, and they need extra time to adequately master basic concepts. Most of my students begin the year lacking the basic prerequisite skills necessary for algebra. Therefore, I must spend an inordinate amount of class time scaffolding instruction to develop students' comprehension and mastery of basic skills.

Integrate key prerequisite skills to the context of larger concepts or skills.

Although it is important to devote this extra time to prerequisite skills, it is critical that an excessive amount of time and effort isn't spent teaching every single skill that students may be lacking. For example, many 9th grade algebra students come to my classroom four to five grade levels behind their peers and cannot proficiently divide or work with fractions. Though I focus on prerequisite skills required to learn new concepts during the year, I do not teach every 4th, 5th, and 6th grade skill students might lack. If I did that, we could never move forward with 9th grade algebra. Instead, I integrate those prerequisite skills into my algebra lessons.

I teach only those skills that are required to master algebra. If a basic knowledge about exponents is needed to do the quadratic formula, then I teach exponents and the quadratic formula at the same time. Rather than teach basic skills at the beginning of the school year to help students get caught up, I instead teach those skills when the more advanced algebra concepts demand them. Similarly, if a 10th grade English teacher has students with no working knowledge of the parts of speech, he or she should continue with the 10th grade requirements, such as reading Shakespeare or writing a persuasive essay. A grammar lesson about the parts of speech can be incorporated into a wider discussion of Shakespeare when such knowledge is critical to comprehension or mastery of 10th grade concepts.

Since everything taught in class must be connected to wider goals and essential standards, CREATE teachers must develop pacing guides catered to individual students' needs. These guides must be based on the essential concepts students must learn during the year, but they also need to allow for the extra time it will take to address necessary prerequisite skills. The table on page 72 provides some guidance on how to begin the process for your own students.

INSTRUCTION SHOULD BE FLEXIBLE

When planning instruction for the school year, flexibility is essential. The timelines I make every year are loose timelines that are inevitably altered by a variety of factors. For example, the testing schedule plays a major role as teachers plan instruction. Urban students generally need more time than traditional populations to prepare for these tests. Issues of culture shock and test anxiety may interfere with the way students perceive test questions or mentally prepare to take exams. Thus, it is important to reserve ample time to review material that will be targeted on the tests and to practice standardized test-taking strategies.

I usually integrate a two- to three-week period into the pacing guide to review released test questions and productive test-taking strategies before my students take the state exam. Again, *your* pacing guide must reflect *your* students' needs and provide them with adequate time to master the essential concepts and demonstrate this learning on high-stakes tests. Identifying released test questions that correspond to key concepts or prerequisite skills will help you integrate this material into your instruction and prepare students early to succeed on the tests. Obviously, it is also helpful to see the direct correlation between the concepts you teach and the material covered on the exam.

ALGEBRA I ESSENTIAL PLANNING

Sample

Key Standards	Textbook Pages/Section	Prerequisite Skills/Teaching Notes	Released Test Questions	Timeline
4.0 *Students simplify expressions prior to solving linear equations and inequalities in one variable, such as* $3(2x-5) + 4(x-2) = 12$	Sections 2.2–2.6	Ability to • add, subtract, multiply, and divide • use the distributive property • solve one-step problems • combine like terms	Released test numbers: 8, 9, 10, 11	August 26–September 25

Key Standards	Textbook Pages/Section	Prerequisite Skills/Teaching Notes	Released Test Questions	Timeline
3.0 *Students solve equations and inequalities involving absolute values.*	Section 11.1	Ability to • evaluate absolute values • solve an inequality	Released test numbers 2, 4, 5	November 18–25

Student learning influences what we teach and when we teach it. In my algebra classes, I usually plan to spend the first two months of school teaching how to simplify expressions and solve equations. My students may realistically need more time to master those concepts. This might be because they lack adequate engagement, feel overwhelmed by the amount of information, or have personal problems that distract them from school. Therefore, I am usually willing to revise my timeline and extend our focus on those concepts accordingly.

I often have to go back to my pacing guide and make minor changes. Sometimes I think of different ways to teach certain concepts so students won't struggle as much. Sometimes I have to eliminate a concept because there is not enough time to teach for mastery. It is important to point out, though, that I won't teach the same few concepts, over and over, for an entire school year. I try my best to get a majority of the class to mastery, and then I move on to the next essential concept. I like to think of teaching as a game where I am the coach and my students are the players. As in most sports, the game rarely turns out as planned, but I have to be willing to adapt my game plan and stay focused on the end goal. In my case, that goal is always to get my students to master as many essential concepts as possible.

Finally, it is important to realize that by focusing only on essential concepts and prerequisites, teachers have more time to be creative and teach concepts that are not in the book. In my classes, I can incorporate social justice ideas or do projects that have high-interest value because I have more time to be creative. The class does not have to be completely geared toward a test. If students are able to master key concepts, I can enrich the learning process with activities that make the content more meaningful and relevant. Even though CREATE teachers need to ensure student mastery of the essential material, they can still be creative and infuse other aspects of learning into the curriculum.

Essentials-focused

PLANNING

KEY POINTS

1 INSTRUCTION MUST REFLECT *Students' Needs*

⟶ **Target** and exclusively focus on mastery of essential concepts.

⟶ **Create** an individualized pacing guide for *your* students.

⟶ **Integrate** prerequisite skills into instruction of essential concepts.

Key Standards: Students solve equations and inequalities involving absolute values.

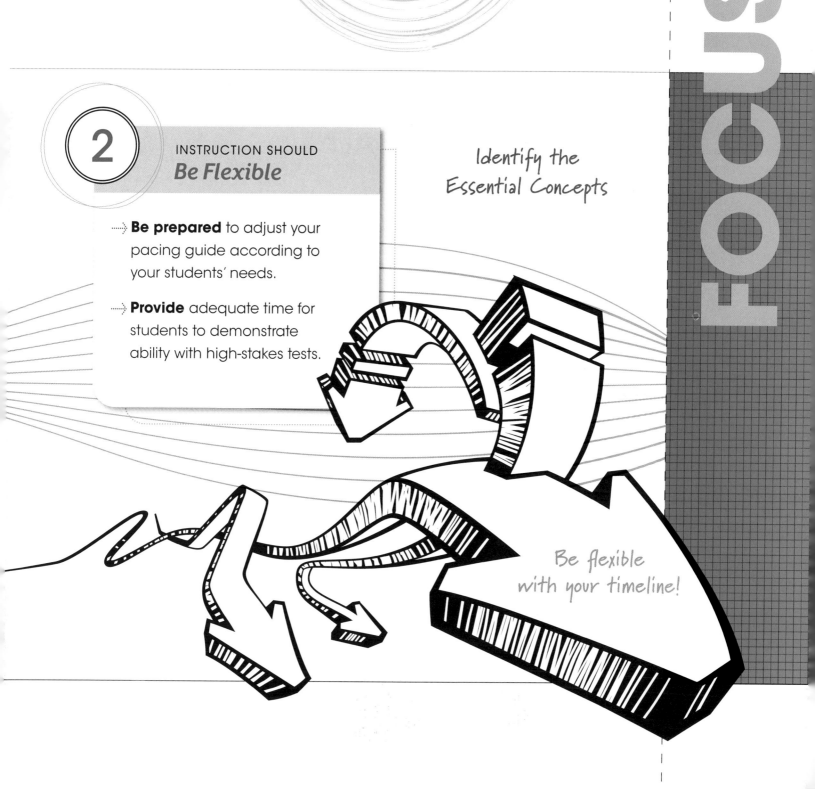

2

INSTRUCTION SHOULD
Be Flexible

┈┈> **Be prepared** to adjust your pacing guide according to your students' needs.

┈┈> **Provide** adequate time for students to demonstrate ability with high-stakes tests.

Identify the
Essential Concepts

Be flexible
with your timeline!

CHAPTER FOUR: *Assessing for Mastery During Class*

Effective instruction is more than good teaching. Likewise, teaching is more than delivering a lesson or covering a textbook. The fourth aspect of the CREATE model is something that is sorely missing from many urban classrooms—using assessment to ensure that students master objectives during class. Checking for understanding is critical to students' success, and assessment is an integral part of instruction because it allows each student and his or her teacher an opportunity to measure student learning and the effectiveness of the teaching.

> A teacher's success is not seen by how much material he or she covers but by how many key concepts students master. Teach only the most essential concepts until mastery!

When it comes right down to it, the effectiveness of any teacher is measured by his or her students' learning. A teacher's success is not seen in how much material he or she has covered but in how many key concepts students have actually mastered (Noguera, 2003). A teacher who simply teaches without assessing would have no idea what students actually know or don't know.

The significance of assessment lies in helping students reach mastery of the objective in class, during class. That last part is key; it should be done during class. Homework should never be the primary tool for concept mastery. I don't proceed to the next chapter or give a test before students convince me that they have mastered what I just taught them. I believe in mastery in class, during class.

LESSON SCAFFOLDING

One part of assessment-driven instruction that is critical to the success of urban students is proper scaffolding. The term *scaffolding* refers to the targeted assistance offered by a teacher (or peer) to support student learning. Scaffolding, when used correctly, is a "bridge used to build upon what students already know to arrive at something they do not" (Benson, 1997, p. 126).

How to Scaffold a Lesson
1. Assess what skills students have already mastered.
2. Break new concepts into realistic steps that target critical foundational skills.
3. Build mastery toward the goal with a step-by-step approach.

It is important to dissect an essential standard or concept into the key component steps necessary for mastery. Before I teach a new concept, I break it down into smaller steps and help students build mastery from where they are. It is important to start with a skill that challenges most students but does not overwhelm them. I must therefore meet students, especially those in the target population, on familiar academic ground and make sure they master each step before advancing.

> "Scaffolding is actually a bridge used to build upon what students already know to arrive at something they do not know."
>
> —BETH BENSON

How is this done? Take, for example, the quadratic formula. In order for students to successfully use the formula to factor equations, they must have mastered many prerequisite skills. These skills include evaluating variables, factoring square roots, calculating exponents, and simplifying expressions. Without a strong grasp of these skills, students will undoubtedly find it difficult to understand or use the quadratic formula. Therefore, I dedicate at least a day to each prerequisite skill until students are ready to tackle the whole quadratic formula. Although the textbook may dictate that the quadratic formula should be taught in one class period, I make necessary revisions according to the specific needs of my students.

I have developed an instructional plan for delivering a lesson so that students master the concept being taught. The OTIS lesson plan for student mastery is a tool that will help you lead your students to mastery during the time that you're together in the classroom.

> Objective
> Teach-back
> Independent Exit Price
> Spiral/Reteach Missed Concepts

OBJECTIVE

A realistic objective for student learning should have two characteristics. First, students must be able to master that objective in one class period. Objectives should not be too grand or heavy that they overwhelm students. For example, "students will do the quadratic formula" is not a good objective if students are learning that formula for the first time. In most urban classrooms where students are below grade level, they might need several days to adequately master the formula. They cannot learn it in one day. A better objective may be to learn how to work with the "4ac" portion of the formula. There is a much better chance that students can master this objective in one class period. Remember: students must feel challenged, but they must still be comfortable and not overwhelmed.

Second, objectives must be specific and measurable. They cannot be something vague or overly broad, such as "students will learn about World War I." Instead, a better objective might be "students will be able to explain five major causes of World War I with 80 percent accuracy." Acceptable objectives should call for students to *prove* they can perform a certain skill with a high degree of accuracy. Likewise, teachers must be able to measure if students can actually perform the appropriate skill or if they have mastered the objective. If an objective is too vague, or if there is no way

Scaffolding for a specific skill is a lot like designing the architecture of a building or tower. You cannot expect students to reach the top in one step, especially if they are below grade level. You must start your lesson "on the ground" from where students are. This is your starting point—the most basic skills students have already mastered. From there, break down the lesson(s) into realistic steps that students can digest, working their way up through foundational skills on their way to the top.

In the following example, the quadratic formula has been broken down in a way that is less intimidating and leads to mastery of each step. In terms of lesson progression, students should work their way "up the tower" from the ground, mastering each step along the way. In other words, teachers present the target skill (the quadratic formula) in practical, "bite-size" chunks.

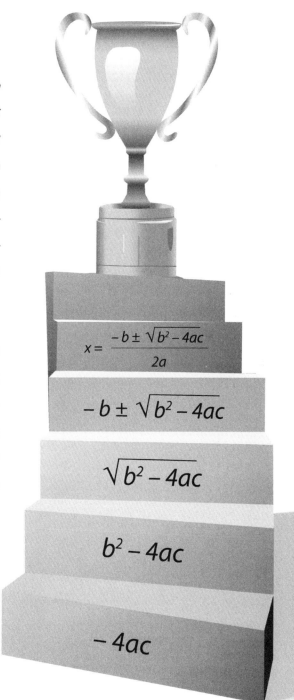

$$x = \frac{-b \pm \sqrt{b^2 - 4ac}}{2a}$$

$$-b \pm \sqrt{b^2 - 4ac}$$

$$\sqrt{b^2 - 4ac}$$

$$b^2 - 4ac$$

$$-4ac$$

for a teacher to assess mastery, there is also no way to gauge the effectiveness of the instruction.

The following are examples of specific, measurable, and "masterable" objectives that can be used across the subject areas:

- Students will be able to explain five major causes of World War I with 80 percent accuracy.

- Students will be able to simplify fractions with 80 percent accuracy.

- Students will be able to conjugate the first-person form of Spanish verbs with 80 percent accuracy.

- Students will be able to write four or five strong thesis statements and three supporting arguments that summarize a writer's position.

TEACH-BACK

The next part of assessment-driven instruction is guided mastery, which demands that teachers explain the material or skills in a way that students can understand. This notion—that teachers must find ways to relate to students' unique learning styles and cultural interests—has been discussed in previous chapters. If teachers teach straight from the textbook and speak a language that seems foreign to students, the lecture will be nothing more than wasted energy. Indeed, teachers who say they are teaching but fail to connect with students and get them to understand are, in essence, talking to themselves.

Once teachers adapt their pedagogy for an urban classroom and students become engaged with a culturally responsive curriculum, it is imperative that teachers remember to check for understanding. The ideal time for this assessment is during the daily lecture; it should not be postponed until the lesson is over. Checks for understanding should become routine and continuous, and they should be used as a litmus test not only for basic comprehension but also for students' ability to independently complete the work. Don't begin teaching Step B until you've assessed understanding of Step A.

These checks can be, and in fact *should* be, informal and quick. It's good practice to never say more than a few sentences without asking a question. The most powerful and effective method of formative assessment I've found is the "teach-back." After I present each concept or step in a problem, I then immediately ask students to repeat this information, or teach the concept, back to the class in their own words. This technique has been used successfully in fields outside of education for many years. For example, according to the American Medical Association, doctors have found that the best way to ensure that patients understand their often complicated medical discussions is through teach-back. Patients are asked to restate, in their own words, the key concepts, decisions, or instructions presented by the doctor (Weiss, 2007). Similarly, the best method for a teacher to know whether students have understood a lecture is to have them reteach and rephrase key concepts.

As I lecture, I constantly ask questions. However, I don't simply ask, "Do you guys get it?" Such a question invites students to tell me they understand and get off the hook, when in reality they are completely lost. Nor do I ask simple *yes* or *no* questions. Instead, I make students explain the steps and teach their classmates (or me) how to do the problem. As a math teacher, for example, I might ask students to teach back a particular step as they graph a line in slope-intercept form. If I were a science teacher, I might ask students to explain the rationale for a specific step of the Krebs

Asking "Do you get it?" invites students to answer in the affirmative (regardless of the truth) and escape accountability. Instead, have individual students demonstrate their understanding of a concept by teaching it back to you.

cycle. If students can confidently teach back a concept with little assistance—and show a sense of ownership—then they are ready to try practice problems on their own.

I want to emphasize another point here. My questioning approach is strategic; I always break up a question into component questions that target smaller steps or related aspects. For example, I can break a particular equation problem into five distinct steps and assess (and reward) a different student for each step. Ultimately, I get multiple students to work together to teach back the solution in a step-by-step manner. Each student builds off a classmate's response, and it becomes a collaborative process with many students involved. Asking one question that targets the final answer would limit my ability to get several kids engaged in the concept.

As part of the process, I ask students to answer questions that I think challenge them but are still appropriate for their respective levels. I therefore differentiate my questions based on individual students' skill levels. I don't want to ask a question that is well below or well above a student's ability. I want to instill confidence and make the student feel like he or she is intelligent and capable of success. By breaking a large question into smaller component questions, I can also assess which particular step is the most difficult or misunderstood.

Don't wait for volunteers; call on students individually. Fire questions at all students and no one can be left out. Everyone has a turn in the "hot seat."

So who should be assessed? The simple answer is everyone, but additional focus should be given to the target population. Don't wait for volunteer hands; call on students individually. Everyone must be in the hot seat at some point. I call on different students to demonstrate understanding during every step of a new concept, but I frequently call on the target population to teach back the concept. It is important to remember that these students may not understand right away. They act out from frustration with the concept,

Break each problem into smaller components.

Use each step as an opportunity to ask a different student a question.

Have students teach back each step of a problem or every key point of a concept.

Ask questions and assess understanding continuously. Make students teach you what they should know.

Assess target population on an individual basis.

Keep them in the hot seat and don't let them escape. Don't wait for volunteers; identify students and call on them.

Personalize your assessment, and ask lots of step-by-step questions to individual students.

Use students' names and ask specific questions. "José, what's the next step?" "Mike, you take over from here." "Tyra, now what do I do?"

or they stay quiet and don't reveal their confusion. I try to prevent either situation from developing in the first place by calling on students by name and asking them to teach back the concept. For example, I'll say, "John, teach me how to solve this equation for 10 points toward your grade." A history teacher might say, "Michelle, tell me what happened as a result of the Lincoln–Douglas debates for 5 points toward your grade."

If students are unable to do the problem or teach back a concept, teachers should be prepared to guide them through the necessary steps. Don't let these students off the hook. Steer them through the relevant points and assess them again. Do this until they are able to teach back the target skill or concept. As an incentive, I offer students points toward their grade and put these points on the board so they feel rewarded publicly. As I ask questions, I reward so many students that there is usually a box with 15 to 20 names on the board by the end of class. If the content is clear and points are at stake, most students will respond if they are called upon to answer a question. For those few who don't (or won't), I may privately assess them at a later point. I won't force one kid to answer if he or she stubbornly refuses to do so.

INDEPENDENT EXIT PRICE

A key element of assessment-driven instruction that comes after students demonstrate mastery of the objective is an independent exit price. An exit price is the most effective way for a teacher to determine whether students mastered the objective and whether they are ready for homework, for a test, or to move on to the next concept.

An exit price is an assignment that forces students to demonstrate understanding through a certain number of problems that must be completed before the end of the class period. A suitable exit price must be rigorous and push students to show mastery of the objective. If students are kept accountable every day, they will work harder and with more urgency—especially if they know there will be a consequence if they don't successfully complete the exit price. Avoid the "easy out." Do not say, "Do as many problems as you can, and do the rest for homework." This doesn't encourage efficient use of class time. Students might take advantage of the situation and take as much time as possible to do one problem. Make them concentrate in class and focus their attention on the daily objectives. Positive pressure is a good thing.

> "In high-achieving schools, teachers persist until they have evidence that students understand key content and are able to demonstrate key skills."
>
> —JOSEPH F. JOHNSON, JR.

Even though a rigorous exit price is important, it is also critical to enforce accountability by monitoring students while they work. During class, I never sit down in my chair. I am always circulating around the room, stopping briefly at each student's desk (especially those of the target population) and making sure students are working on the appropriate assignment, including the exit price. Students may say they understand and don't need you to monitor them. Don't believe them. Circulate and tenaciously monitor all students as they work on the exit price. Most important, you must grade the exit price assignment during class and assign a consequence if a student fails.

> Circulate around the classroom and tenaciously monitor all students as they work on the exit price. This is their opportunity to demonstrate what they know.

Consider the following analogy. If you teach someone how to drive a car, you cannot accurately tell whether he or she knows how to drive by asking questions alone. That person must physically be able to drive from point A to point B. He or she needs to have time and an opportunity to demonstrate an ability to sit behind the wheel and drive. The road test at the end of a driving lesson is the exit price. Only after someone has proven an ability to drive from point A to point B independently should he or she be allowed to do "homework" and drive alone or take a driving test.

Typically, people remember only 10 to 20 percent of what they hear, but with practice and repetition, they remember (and learn) 80 to 90 percent of what they do and say (Tiberius & Tipping, 1990). To learn anything well, students need to perform a task multiple times—independently, if possible. Therefore, practice in the classroom—in the form of an independent exit price—is the most effective way for students to internalize a concept and for teachers to assess students' understanding of that concept.

Always pose questions (during teach-back and on the exit price) that target different students' abilities. A good rule of thumb is that 20 percent of your questions should target those students with the lowest skill levels and 20 percent should target the most advanced students in class. The remaining 60 percent should address the "average" level of student proficiency.

The exit price should be achievable by all students. For advanced students, I may include extra-credit problems that are slightly more difficult. If these students finish the additional problems early (or don't want to do them), then I ask them to help their classmates (and offer them extra points for doing so). Every day in my algebra class, I assign an exit price that measures how well my students understand the objective. My students must hand in this exit price, or, at the very least, I have to grade it before they leave. This process introduces accountability for learning the objective since I can accurately tell if my students can do the problems by themselves.

If students independently demonstrate that they can complete the exit price, then the teacher can safely conclude that they learned the objective and that the teaching was effective. If students nod their heads in agreement throughout the whole period but cannot complete the exit price by themselves, then the teaching was not as effective as the teacher perhaps thought it was and the objective was not met. Consequences and necessary next steps are discussed later.

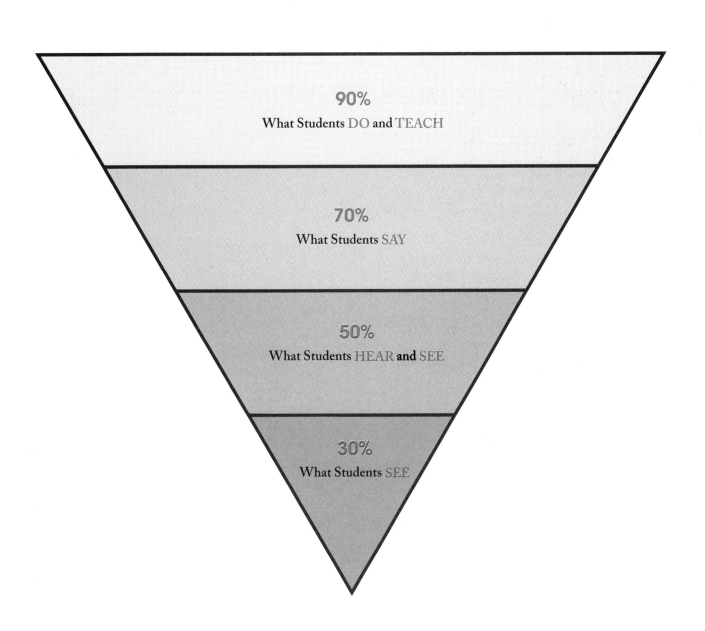

90%
What Students DO and TEACH

70%
What Students SAY

50%
What Students HEAR and SEE

30%
What Students SEE

While an independent exit price is an excellent opportunity for teachers to assess student understanding and identify areas of instruction that students did not grasp, it is also important to provide enough time for students to complete the exit price. In other words, teachers cannot lecture for 45 minutes and leave only five minutes for the exit price. The exit price must be rigorous, but students need sufficient time to practice on their own.

> Here is how I divide a 50-minute class period:
>
> 10 minutes: attendance, announcements, warm-up exercise that builds on the previous day's objective and previews the current day's objective
>
> 20 minutes: lecture with interactive teach-back
>
> 20 minutes: independent practice and exit price demonstration

Students must be kept accountable for finishing the exit price. Inherent in this is that teachers need to tenaciously monitor students while they work on the assignment. Teachers cannot sit down and hide behind the desk. The chair is illegal. I don't want any kid to fail, so I continually circulate to all students, make sure they are working on the exit price, and provide immediate feedback. I never believe students who say they do not need any help. If I did, it would be far too easy for them to escape notice and shed their accountability. Consistent, immediate feedback is a powerful tool that raises student performance (Marzano et al., 2001).

Grade the exit price *in class* as you circulate around the room.

The final step in this process is to grade the exit price papers in class. This deserves repeating: *Grade the exit price in class.* Do not take 150 papers home to grade. If I did that every day, I would get nothing else done! Grade them as you circulate around the room. In my class, exit price papers are usually worth 50 points. I don't

ACHIEVING INDEPENDENT MASTERY

<table>
<tr>
<td>

20 minutes
lecture with interactive teach-back

"Show me you can do the problem
if I guide you."

</td>
<td>

20 minutes
independent practice and exit price demonstration

"Prove that you can do it alone
correctly before you leave."

</td>
</tr>
</table>

MAINTAINING STUDENT ACCOUNTABILITY

"You need to correctly write 10 thesis statements before class is over, or you'll miss basketball practice and redo the assignment after school."

"You need to write a paragraph explaining the causes of the Civil War before you leave, or I'll have to call your coach."

grade every problem. I look at just enough problems, especially the essential problems, and judge what level of mastery that student has reached. If the student reaches 80 percent (or higher) mastery, I award an *A* for the day. If only 70 percent mastery was achieved, he or she gets a *C*. It's critical that I look at enough problems to judge fairly the level of mastery that each student reaches for the day.

By the time guided mastery through interactive teach-back is over, you should be sure that at least 80 percent of your students are ready to show mastery on the independent exit price while still in class. If they cannot show mastery on the exit price by themselves, then you must rethink how to improve your approach to guided mastery.

After I grade each exit price paper in class, I immediately communicate that grade to the student. This immediacy sends the message that I am serious about the work they do, and I'm not just assigning busy work. In this way, I'm able to tell students if they got an *A* and can leave or if they failed and have to redo the work as a consequence. I make it very difficult and uncomfortable for students to go out the door without mastering the day's objective.

Teachers must make it clear that there will be consequences for students who do not finish the exit price. If a student does not demonstrate mastery of the day's objective (I draw the line at 70 percent accuracy on the exit price), that student receives an *F* for the day. There is then an immediate consequence, such as the requirement to make up the exit price after school or during lunch. It is essential that these consequences are carried out. Students must feel that if they do not complete the exit price appropriately, the teacher will be on their case.

How do teachers enforce these consequences? Parents and coaches should be used as allies in the effort to reach and motivate students. A parent, coach, or guardian is often the most significant person in a student's life. If a student wastes time and does not finish the exit price, I will call his or her parent, coach, or grandparent and

"Jim was able to complete 20 out of 25 Spanish conjugations before the end of class. He mastered the objective."

"Mike could not write 10 strong similes. He did not master the objective."

You must define what mastery looks like depending on the day's objective and type of assignment. Grade the exit price during class and tell the students what grade they earned before class is over. It is crucial to keep the kids accountable and make them prove they can do the objective on the independent exit price.

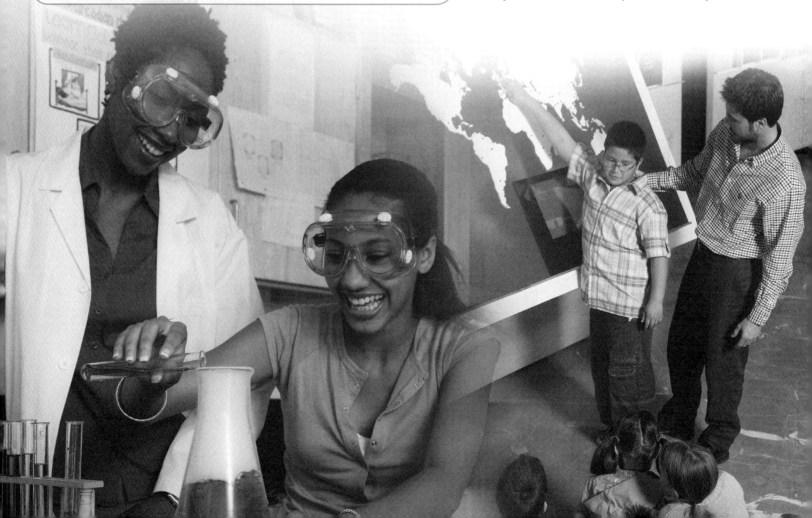

demand that the student stays after school or spends time during lunch to finish the work. By any measure, I am hard on my students. Just as my students know that I will hold them accountable to their learning contracts, they also know that the same consequences will apply if they fail to complete their exit price adequately. They will certainly test me, and, within the first few weeks of school, I inevitably catch some of them goofing off and not working on their exit price. I have no qualms about a student missing football practice because I kept him after school. Students tend to work hard almost every day once they see that the teacher is "not playin'." Be tenacious about keeping students accountable for mastery in class!

> It is essential that consequences are carried out. Students must feel a sense of urgency to complete the exit price appropriately. There can be no escape from mastery.

Why am I so hard on my students? What about those kids who actually try hard but are unable to achieve 70 percent mastery due to a low skill level or learning disability? I refuse to lower the standard. I circulate around the classroom and specifically help those kids who are struggling with their work. I also enlist more advanced students to help their struggling classmates. There should be no excuse for a student to fail the exit price. If, even after getting help and trying hard, they still fail to achieve 70 percent accuracy, I let them know they have to come after school or during lunch, get help from me, and redo the exit price. Most students respond to these tough measures when they see that I diligently enforce the consequences. This "tough love" is how I ensure that each student reaches mastery at every step along the way and that no child gets left behind.

> There is too much room for error and uncertainty with homework. Assess student mastery during class with individual attention, an interactive teach-back process, and an independent exit price.

Some teachers believe in lecturing for 45 minutes and giving homework as the primary tool for assessment and independent practice. In my opinion, this is one of

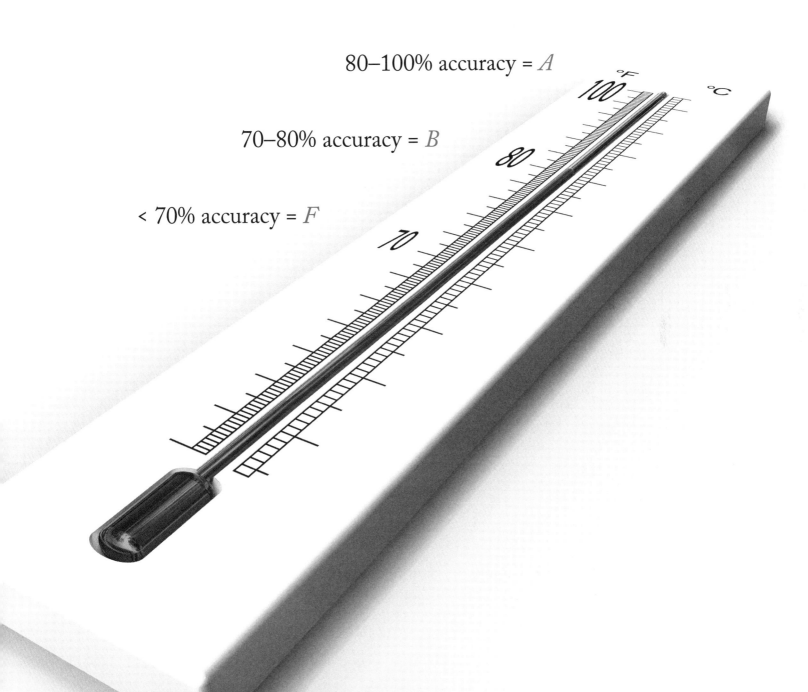

80–100% accuracy = A

70–80% accuracy = B

< 70% accuracy = F

the biggest mistakes teachers in urban classrooms can make. Homework should *not* be used as the primary assessment tool. The most effective time and place to assess student mastery and provide constructive feedback is in class, during class.

There is too much room for error and uncertainty with homework. Students might do the problems all wrong, which will only reinforce incorrect information and faulty strategies. Students might copy a friend's work and turn it in as their own. There is also the high possibility that students may not even do the homework in the first place. In my experience, only about 20 percent of any class actually gives an appropriate amount of time and attention to homework assignments. Therefore, because it forces students to do the work in class and turn it in, an independent exit price is the best way to assess whether students truly understand the material. Homework can be assigned for extra practice after students have adequately demonstrated mastery in class.

SPIRAL/RETEACH MISSED CONCEPTS

So far, we have discussed guided mastery through interactive teach-back and independent mastery through the exit price. What if students fail the exit price? What then? If only a few students are affected, I typically enforce consequences such as lunchtime or after-school tutoring. However, if *many* students fail the exit price, then I am forced to go back and examine what *I* did wrong. What could have caused so many students to fail the exit price and not achieve mastery of the day's objective? Was the objective overwhelming? Was the exit price misaligned with the objective? Was the classroom environment too disruptive? Depending on the circumstances, I then revise my approach and make whatever adjustments are necessary.

If students do not reach mastery, reflect on the effectiveness of your teaching strategies.

For example, if students didn't understand a particular concept because I taught "over their heads," then I need to think of a better approach to teach that concept.

"I did my homework, but I didn't learn anything!"

"I did my homework, but I copied my friends'."

"I did my homework, but it's all wrong."

"I didn't do my homework."

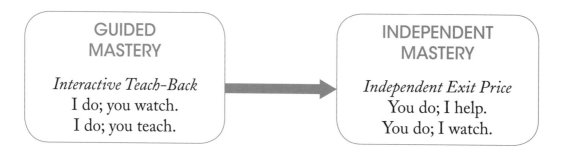

I immediately address the problem and reteach the essential objective in a different way the next day. I refuse to move on to the next essential concept (or to blame my students) if a majority of them continue to struggle. I also spiral the missed essential concept into the next day's exit price. This means that concepts missed on Monday will also show up on Tuesday's exit price. Students remain accountable and should not escape responsibility for missed concepts.

This is an important strategy to practice regardless of specific difficulties. A typical exit price in my math class has 20 questions on the current objective and 15 questions on other essential concepts that students must not forget. By making students practice those essential concepts over and over, I make sure they retain what they have learned throughout the year.

SPIRALING ESSENTIALS ON THE EXIT PRICE

60% of questions are
new essentials that tie into the day's objective

40% of questions are
previously taught essentials students shouldn't forget

Assessing for Mastery

DURING CLASS

Independent Mastery

A 80–100%

B 70–80%

F <70%

KEY POINTS

Scaffold instruction to meet students on familiar academic ground.

Establish specific, measurable, and "masterable" learning objectives.

Have students teach back important concepts to demonstrate understanding.

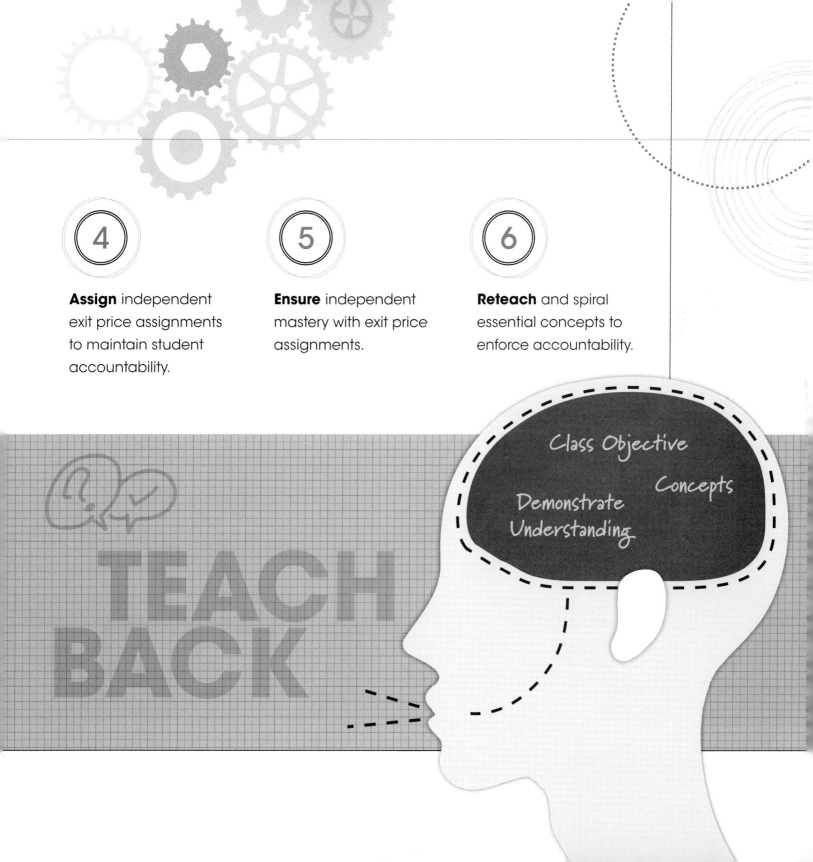

4

Assign independent exit price assignments to maintain student accountability.

5

Ensure independent mastery with exit price assignments.

6

Reteach and spiral essential concepts to enforce accountability.

TEACH BACK

Class Objective

Concepts

Demonstrate Understanding

CHAPTER FIVE: *Test Models*

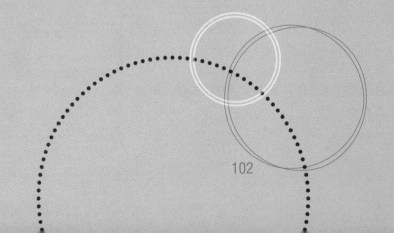

The fifth aspect of the CREATE model is exposing students to test models and test-taking strategies. Most teachers have taught students who know math or history material in the classroom but fail a high-stakes test. Therefore, if we are to do justice to our students—especially the target population—and arm them with the tools to survive and compete in the real world, then we must help them succeed on standardized exams.

Culturally responsive instruction, rigorous expectations, and assessment of essential concepts are critical elements of urban student success. Even though urban students may be exposed to quality instruction and understand the content, they might still be unable to succeed on state and national standardized tests. Although there is much debate over the use of standardized tests, it is clear that these tests are not going to disappear. CREATE teachers, therefore, must prepare their students to demonstrate and apply knowledge on standardized tests.

INHERENT BIASES OF STANDARDIZED TESTS

Test preparation is significant because standardized tests are used as a major indicator of whether students are proficient in core subjects. National tests such as the SAT and ACT affect college entrance decisions, and graduate school entrance exams such as the GRE not only affect graduate school admissions but also are taken into account by many potential employers. It is important to prepare students for these kinds of tests because, even though students may understand the content *on* the test, they may not understand the structure *of* the test. In other words, students might be proficient in math, but they may fail the test because they aren't familiar with a particular test type or manner in which a question is asked. In this light, it is imperative that teachers of urban students ensure that their students are not at a disadvantage when they take standardized exams.

This issue of cultural bias on standardized exams has been the subject of much discussion, and tests such as the SAT college entrance exam have been declared to be culturally biased against minorities. The College Board (the organization that develops and publishes the SAT) submits all questions to a rigorous and extensive testing and approval process that allows test makers to know in advance how students will perform on each question. According to the Princeton Review Foundation, however, the final test is often composed of questions that "favor" Caucasian students, who are more likely than minorities to answer those questions correctly. For the October 2000 exam, none of the questions that favored minority students (as evidenced during the testing and approval process) were selected for the final version. Studies have shown that 54 percent of Caucasian students answer SAT questions correctly, but only 40 percent of African American students achieve the same result (Young, 2003). If the College Board were to select questions that decreased this gap in scores, then minorities' success with standardized exams could actually improve—along with their qualifications for college. Indeed, when test stimuli are more culturally pertinent to the experiences of African Americans, their performance improves (Hayles, 1991).

According to Alfie Kohn, "noninstructional factors explain most of the variance among test scores when schools or districts are compared" (Kohn, 2000). He concludes that test results are significantly affected by a combination of four variables: number of parents living at home, parents' educational backgrounds, community in which students live, and poverty rate. Other critics argue that many standardized tests require proficiency with specific knowledge and skills that favors students from certain cultural backgrounds. Assessment bias, according to W. James Popham, "occurs whenever test items offend or unfairly penalize students for reasons related to students' personal characteristics,

"[Standardized testing] is a game that a lot of kids—predominantly kids of color—simply cannot win."

—ALFIE KOHN

Urban students of color may automatically be at an academic disadvantage due to test bias that exists on standardized exams. We need to prepare students to succeed on these tests despite the inequities and biases that may exist.

"I studied so hard. I know this stuff! But I don't understand this question!"

"You taught me everything...but it's not on this test!! What is the question asking? I quit!!"

such as their race, gender, ethnicity, religion, or socioeconomic status . . . . A test can be biased if it *offends* students or if it *unfairly penalizes* students because of students' personal characteristics" (Popham, 2003, p. 55).

Jay Rosner, executive director of the Princeton Review Foundation, examined answers from thousands of SAT test takers and analyzed the responses in context with students' race, ethnicity, and gender. His findings showed that "every single question carefully preselected to appear on the test favors whites over blacks" (Rosner, 2003). What does this mean? It means that a higher percentage (sometimes considerably higher) of white students answered a particular question correctly. His conclusion is that the SAT is a white-preference test, and he is not alone in this assessment.

Our urban students of color may automatically be at a disadvantage due to test bias that exists on standardized exams, but we can do better. We need to prepare students to succeed on these tests *despite* the inequities and biases that may exist.

> "The aim of test-taking skills training is to improve the overall *validity* of the test by making scores more accurately reflect what students really know."
>
> —THOMAS SCRUGGS & MARGO MASTROPIERI

TEST PREPARATION

Test preparation is crucial because many urban students have internalized the notion that they cannot succeed on tests and in school. If they escape from tests or are told they cannot perform well on tests, their expectations are lowered, which will simply reinforce their own feelings of inadequacy. In addition, some African American youth reject success as "white behavior" or because it is something that would please the teacher—their perceived enemy. This rejection by some African American students may reflect an unwillingness or inability to set realistic goals, the influence of negative peer pressure, or a diminished lack of motivation (Kuykendall, 1989). Whatever the cause, the results are the same: low self-image, fear of failure, lack of motivation, and lack of all desire to even try for success.

By contrast, students who strive for success, have high levels of self-worth, and consistently set high standards for themselves are more likely to overcome (or learn from) failure. Therefore, teachers should take an aggressive role in encouraging and supporting urban students to believe they can succeed on tests. If urban students can demonstrate their understanding on tests and assessments, then they will have defied the stereotype that says they cannot perform well on exams. By exposing students to test models and the specific questioning styles of standardized tests, teachers can effectively build student confidence and foster the belief that students can succeed on tests they may have feared in the past.

Help students become familiar with the language of and question types commonly found on standardized exams. When students are comfortable with these tests, you can accurately assess if they learned the content. In terms of instructional value, failure from a lack of comprehension is more helpful than failure due to an inability to understand and answer a question.

"The aim of test-taking skills training is to improve the overall *validity* of the test by making scores more accurately reflect what students really know. This is done by making sure that students lose points *only* because they do not know the information, and not for some reason unrelated to content knowledge, such as marking an answer choice incorrectly, or misinterpreting the test directions" (Scruggs & Mastropieri, 1992, p. 4). Indeed, if students understand the structure and format of a test, then it follows that they can more efficiently demonstrate their learning. Inexperienced test takers may know the content assessed by a particular question but still answer incorrectly because they do not understand the question type. Conversely, students with previous exposure to standardized tests and test-taking skills are more likely to answer a question incorrectly *only* if they are unfamiliar with the content, not because the test format is confusing or intimidating.

Students of all social and cultural backgrounds must be encouraged to regard failure as a learning experience. The confidence that grows out of consistent encouragement will make it easier for struggling students to persist and use failure constructively. Successful performance on standardized tests will do wonders to raise their self-confidence and self-esteem.

In sports, athletes usually play in a scrimmage before an actual game. We should give our students the same kind of practice and preparation before a high-stakes test. Ideally, by the time students take a high-stakes test, it should appear easy and familiar. Therefore, teachers should frequently expose their students to standardized test models. As I plan my instructional pacing guide at the beginning of the school year, I make sure to integrate time to prepare students for the tests they'll take. I identify released test questions that correspond to the key concepts I'm teaching and then integrate model test questions into most of my exit price assignments, well in advance of major state and national tests. These preview questions help familiarize students with test format, language, and expectations. It's important to do this early and daily so students have sufficient practice. I spend at least one month reviewing test models before students have to take a standardized test. By the time they take the test, they feel prepared because they are familiar with the types of questions they will face.

> Integrate model test questions into exit price assignments. These preview questions help familiarize students with test format, language, and expectations.

In addition to including model test questions on exit price assignments, I spend at least two to three weeks reviewing released test questions that students *can* and *should* be able to answer but may need extra help understanding. I spend extra time reviewing and

A TYPICAL TEST QUESTION

Solve: $4x + 23 - 2x + 23 = -4$

Line 1: $2x + 46 = -4$

Line 2: $2x = 42$

Line 3: $x = 21$

Which of the following statements is true?

A. Line 1 is the first incorrect line.
B. Line 2 is the first incorrect line.
C. Line 3 is the first incorrect line.
D. All lines are correct.

Questions like this lead many urban students to throw up their hands in frustration and exclaim, "*What are you asking??*" Let's give our students the opportunity to showcase their learning and compete in the real world by preparing them to succeed on their tests.

reteaching those concepts that students may have forgotten or need extra practice with. I don't spend time teaching my students how to do every problem that might appear on the test. Some questions may not relate to the essential concepts we've covered in class, or some may be very difficult and would require so much of the students' time and attention that they wouldn't have time to devote to questions they *can* and *should* be able to answer.

Nevertheless, most test questions will relate to the key concepts, and my students should be able to do them if they are prepared to read and comprehend the questions. It would be unfair if students knew the content but never had a chance to demonstrate this learning because they were completely unfamiliar with the format or style of a test question. I therefore pick and choose my battles. I prepare students to win realistic battles with the knowledge, skills, and experience they possess.

About a month before the test, I give students mock exams or practice tests that look exactly like the standardized test they will take. I typically make this an exit price assignment and keep students accountable for completing the tests. We discuss numerous test-taking strategies such as process of elimination, educated guessing, and pacing. I always tell students to focus on the questions they really know and not spend too much time on the most difficult questions. Ultimately, my goal is simply to give my students a chance to demonstrate their knowledge and feel proud of themselves.

Test Models

1 **Avoid** the inherent biases of standardized tests with exposure and practice.

2 **Frequently expose** students to test models in the classroom.

3 **Practice** test-taking strategies.

4 **Help** students feel prepared for and comfortable with standardized tests.

Prepare students to win realistic battles with the knowledge, skills, and experience they possess.

PRACTICE

CHAPTER SIX: *Extra One-on-One Tutoring*
for Struggling Students

This chapter briefly discusses the importance of individualized, one-on-one assistance for struggling students. This aspect of the CREATE model stresses the importance of providing extra help for the target population. Despite culturally responsive instruction, step-by-step personal assessment, a rigorous exit price, and exposure to test models and test-taking strategies, a few kids may still be left behind. These students require additional one-on-one attention, which could take place during class, during a nonacademic period such as lunch, or after school.

According to Robert Slavin, "the most difficult problem of school and classroom organization is accommodating instruction to the needs of students with different levels of prior knowledge and different learning rates" (1995). If a heterogeneous class sits through a lesson on long division, for example, some students may fail to learn the material because they have not yet mastered the prerequisite skills of subtraction, multiplication, or simple division. If the instructional pace is too rapid, these students will be left behind. Also, many students seem to get distracted in a large class by their peers and cannot focus as well. I have a few students who are very bright but cannot focus for more than a few minutes at a time because they *have* to say something to someone. These students are highly distractible and literally cannot block out the sight or sounds of their peers. Some of my students have been diagnosed with attention deficit disorder (ADD) or attention deficit hyperactivity disorder (ADHD) and struggle to sit still for more than a few consecutive minutes. Students who process information more slowly than others may therefore become lost in a class that is seemingly paced too fast.

How can teachers provide individualized attention to students who need extra help? As discussed earlier, I am able to devote one-on-one time to struggling students as they work on their exit price because I am constantly moving around and monitoring their work. As I circulate among the target population, I am able to help kids individually and clarify concepts for students who would have been lost without this individualized help.

One-on-one tutoring can be used as a consequence for students who don't pay attention or learn the objective during class.

"I should have paid attention in class! I better learn this or I'll have to stay tomorrow also."

ONE-ON-ONE TUTORING

One-on-one tutoring enables me to help students by modeling and demonstrating concepts in a manner that accommodates each student's unique learning style. During one-on-one tutoring, a teacher can embrace varying styles, teach in ways that students fully understand, and unlock previous learning challenges (Bloom, 1984). Furthermore, one-on-one tutoring facilitates direct instruction. Sometimes called mastery learning, direct instruction emphasizes clearly defined tasks and incremental growth, allowing students to master each lesson before moving forward.

Direct instruction has been widely studied, field tested, and implemented in urban environments, including the Baltimore Curriculum Project (BCP) in Baltimore city public schools. According to BCP, "Direct instruction is used to help students gain the basic reading, writing and mathematics skills they will need before proceeding to the more advanced curriculum.... [Direct instruction takes] nothing for granted. Teachers make no assumptions about what children have learned or will learn outside of school. All necessary skills are taught in the classroom" (Baltimore Curriculum Project, n.d.).

One-on-one tutoring facilitates direct instruction, which emphasizes clearly defined tasks and incremental growth, allowing students to master each lesson before moving forward.

With one-on-one tutoring, teachers or tutors can reteach (review) lessons and reread (clarify) material, thereby helping students master the subject matter. In my classes, learning improves at a much faster pace than in a one-to-thirty lecture-based environment since I am concentrating and focusing on individual students and can detect the sources of confusion much more efficiently. Once I identify the problems, I can address them immediately. For example, many of my students have a really hard time adding negative numbers. I structure my lessons to teach this basic skill at these students' existing level and help them tackle the other 80 percent of the lesson or exit price, which may be more advanced. Despite the differentiated approach of my lecture, those students might still have difficulty adding negative numbers and applying the correct sign(s). More intense individual tutoring enables me to detect the exact nature of their confusion—there may be several areas of confusion that are not clear until I sit down and dissect an individual student's thinking process. As a result of this personalized instruction, I can more accurately monitor how well students are mastering the lessons, and I can then adapt the pace and targeting of skills accordingly.

One-on-one tutoring, by its very nature, also demands that students spend more time on task. I don't need to remind students to focus or reprimand them for talking or interrupting other students because there are not 30 other kids around them. In a one-on-one, individualized environment, it is much easier to focus and the learning inevitably becomes more efficient. The same student who struggled for 50 minutes during class to understand how to add negative numbers may need only 10 minutes of individualized attention after school. Again, I can diagnose the problem quickly and repair it immediately.

> Some students *need* extra one-on-one attention that is absent of all other distractions. Use lunch periods and after-school hours to provide this individualized help.

SUPERSTAR TUTORS

Unfortunately (yet inevitably), I am not able to help everyone who needs one-on-one tutoring; therefore, I use my best students to collaborate and help those who are struggling. I identify "superstar tutors" whom I can call on to help other kids. Superstar tutors are my allies in the classroom, and they can be an immense help as I address the individual needs of certain students. When these students are done with their own work, I ask them to pair with and help their struggling classmates, and I award them extra points for the assignment. As much as possible, I intentionally seat tutors and struggling students next to each other to make the tutoring process easier and less disruptive. I instruct and encourage my tutors to help their classmates understand the material without simply giving them the answers.

Superstar tutors can and should be your allies in the classroom.

No other strategy changes the classroom dynamic as profoundly as cooperative work. Most students don't feel connected to one another without cooperative work, and there is a sense of tension and isolation that exists when 30 kids are always individually working. When students work in pairs or small groups, however, learning becomes active and personalized. Struggling students benefit from seeing how more advanced students solve problems and approach class material. Conversely, advanced students support and reinforce their knowledge by "playing teacher" and expressing their thinking processes and the material in their own words. Interestingly, studies by Cynthia Rohrbeck reveal that peer-tutoring interventions are more effective for students in urban settings, students from disadvantaged socioeconomic backgrounds, and minority students (Rohrbeck, Ginsburg-Block, Fantuzzo, & Miller, 2003).

I identify potential tutors based on advanced skill levels and the maturity to get along with and help peers. With this in mind, I discourage unfriendly or confrontational students from acting as superstar tutors. I do my best to match tutors with students who will try hard and not give too much resistance. Tutors are instructed not to use negative or derogatory language but, instead, to only use positive and supportive language. If tutors violate this understanding, they forfeit their role as superstar tutors, and I may even subtract points from their grades, depending on the severity of the violation.

If a particular student is not receptive to a tutor's help, I encourage the tutor to help another student. I will occasionally ask tutors to check on particular students and compare answers. It is important to avoid elevating the tutor in the class's eye. I don't want to

HOW TO PROVIDE ONE-ON-ONE TUTORING TO STRUGGLING STUDENTS

1. Constantly circulate around the classroom and help struggling students individually.

2. Consistently use "superstar tutors" to help their classmates after their own work is complete.

3. Aggressively make students attend additional tutoring sessions outside of class.

make it look like a tutor is superior to the students he or she is helping. To this end, I will promote the notion of collaboration and say that I want people to check one another's answers. It is also critical that tutors don't simply give answers. Instead, they must help students identify their mistakes and figure out the answers for themselves.

Many people have asked me how I train these students. The truth is that I don't formally train them; I just give them a few pointers before I ask them to help their struggling classmates. "Superstar tutor" is not an official job, nor is peer tutoring a daily event. Some days, it might only take 5–10 minutes, assuming the advanced students have this much time remaining after they finish their own work.

INDIVIDUAL TUTORING OUTSIDE OF CLASS

I also spend time during lunch periods and after school to provide additional one-on-one assistance to those students who need it. If you recall, I make it mandatory for students who fail an exit price to come to one of these sessions, and I try my best to ensure that those students actually come. As I look at exit price assignments, I might see that certain students routinely make the same mistakes. It's usually easy to recognize that these students need additional one-on-one help to understand a particular concept.

Make individual tutoring mandatory. Do not give students an option; they must come after school or during a free period.

Many students learn better and are only able to focus when they are not surrounded by their peers. I have found that even five minutes of individual help can sometimes clarify a concept and be a breakthrough to student success. As I've mentioned, individual tutoring allows students to work without distractions, and it allows me to more easily identify specific areas of need and address them. Finally, the extra tutoring convinces kids that their teacher really cares. Personally, I have seen students become more motivated when they see my dedication, and they, in turn, become more willing to give me some of their time after school or on weekends.

Another benefit of one-on-one tutoring is that it establishes a close relationship between teacher and student. I usually tutor students four days out of the week for at least an hour. Usually, this is done during lunch, after school, or on weekends. Sometimes, though, I may go to a student's home if he or she is unable to get a ride home after school. The individual attention that comes with this tutoring allows for a high level of quality interaction. If the teacher is tenacious about providing individualized attention, students quickly recognize and appreciate that the teacher really cares. This tutoring allows me to help students with their math skills, but it also establishes a relationship of care and trust. Once students are convinced that I really care about their learning, their behavior and effort in class also improves.

One final issue that teachers need to factor in to the tutoring equation is tardiness and absenteeism. Students may get sick and miss an important class or lesson, or students might get suspended and miss several days in a row. I don't believe in punishing students by letting them fall further behind and then fail as a result. Instead, I encourage those students to come for extra help during lunch or after school so I can help them individually. If they don't miss any of the material, then they won't be lost when the class moves on and proceeds with the next lesson. Usually, the relationship I forge with my students from the beginning of the year helps to ensure their willingness to come. I rarely have to fight a student to get him or her to come for individualized help when it's necessary. If a student resists, and it is a struggle to get him or her to come for extra help, then I don't hesitate to call the parents or a coach, as I have repeatedly mentioned.

The key point to take away from this is that urban educators *must* make time to help struggling students on a one-on-one basis. If this can be done during class, fantastic; however, it will more than likely require time outside of class, during lunch, or after school.

Extra One-on-One Tutoring

FOR STRUGGLING STUDENTS

1 **Provide** additional, individualized tutoring both in and out of class.

 **2** **Integrate** cooperative work to the classroom with peer-tutoring activities.

3 **Ensure** that students who need help actually receive it.

 **4** **Use** additional tutoring as a consequence for unacceptable behavior.

SUPERSTAR
TUTORS!

No other strategy
changes the classroom
dynamic as profoundly as
cooperative work.

EXTRA HELP

CONCLUSION: *Making the CREATE Model Work for You*

The CREATE instructional model can help you unlock the potential that exists within your students, but the impact it can have in urban classrooms is also influenced by the academic culture that permeates the entire school. Therefore, even though teachers who take personal responsibility for their students' success can implement the model effectively, there are other institutional factors that may affect their success with students.

First and foremost, the administration must support teachers and the instructional approach that is put forth in the CREATE model. Teachers must be allowed to emphasize mastery of essentials and adjust the pacing guide according to the unique needs of their students. Similarly, the administration must accept the use of a culturally responsive curriculum, and teachers who use rewards (as emphasized by CREATE) to motivate students should also feel supported by their leadership.

I have been in inner-city schools where students were allowed to roam the halls and come to class when and if they felt like it. No matter what I did, I could not overcome the deleterious effect of a negative school culture. The school culture *must* provide a positive climate for learning. Students must always feel that they are in a safe environment for learning, that there are high expectations for behavior and academic achievement, and that they are held accountable for their actions. Attendance and behavioral policies must be apparent and enforced. If the school is out of control, chaotic, and unsafe, students cannot learn even if teachers are dedicated and caring. If there is no expectation on students to come to class, or if truancy policies aren't enforced, then teachers might find themselves standing at the front of empty classrooms.

Interventions should also be in place for those students whom no teacher can reach because of behavioral or truancy issues. If there are two or three students who are failing their classes and constantly distracting other students, the school must have a plan to deal with those students. As I indicated earlier, I recognize that I cannot save every student. I cannot save the student who only comes to class once a week. I cannot save the student who refuses to do any work, despite my best efforts to develop a personal relationship. Although only a few students fit this description, I acknowledge that they do exist. Therefore, it is imperative that the school has a supportive administration and effective intervention system to deal with the most difficult students. Schools cannot turn a blind eye and allow a few difficult students to corrupt the rest of the students who come to class and dedicate themselves to learning.

I must reiterate that I would never write off a student until I have personally tried multiple interventions to engage him or her. If the struggling student is doing well in other classes, then I make sure to talk to his or her other teachers and find out what they do to engage the student. This is rarely the case, however—it is rare for a student to fail my class but succeed in another. A student who is disrupting or failing my class is usually a behavioral issue in every class. In extreme cases, I expect the school leadership to enforce accountability on students who consistently disrupt every class they are in.

Finally, student achievement must be glamorized throughout the school. Even though the academic climate must be rigorous, the physical environment should make student success seem "cool." For example, hang portraits of students who made the greatest progress and hold school assemblies to recognize student success. The overall school climate affects what happens inside individual classrooms—positively *and* negatively. The CREATE model has the greatest impact in a positive school culture that values positive citizenship and student achievement.

FREQUENTLY ASKED QUESTIONS

I hope this book has been a valuable tool and that you will continue to use it as a resource for helping your students. There is a self-evaluation checklist at the end of this chapter that will help you identify which of your current teaching practices align with the CREATE model. Use this checklist as you plan your lessons. Make copies of it and take notes as you continue to develop and refine the process that works best for your students.

Before I draw to a close, though, I would like to address some questions that may still be in your mind. The following FAQ includes some of the most common questions that people ask when I give presentations about the CREATE model. Although I still have a lot to learn myself, these are my frank responses to those recurring questions.

How do you create lessons that are culturally responsive and have an exit price?

I typically spend 40–45 minutes each day to create a lesson plan for the subject I will teach the following day. I plan an objective based on where my students are in terms of mastering the essential concepts, which I have already mapped out in a timeline. The objective is simple and something that I can assess for mastery on an exit price. I put myself in my students' shoes and ask myself, "What will it take to understand this objective during the lecture?" I integrate students' interests, sports, music, and familiar vocabulary to hook their attention to the lesson plan. I ask myself if students will understand the lesson the way I intend to explain it. The more relevant and connected the curriculum or lesson is to the students, the more they will be engaged with it. Moreover, I think about what it would take for students to be ready to tackle and master the exit price that I assign. The lectures I plan are interactive and involve students, particularly those in the target population, teaching the concept back to me or the class.

Although the delivery of instruction is important, I spend a majority of my planning time designing an appropriate exit price—one which assesses whether students have learned the essential concept(s) at the heart of the day's lesson. My exit price assignments usually consist of 20 questions that cover new material from the day and at least 10–15 more questions that focus on previously taught concepts. This latter group of questions almost always includes the most recent concepts that students need to know. I also make it a point to target areas of weakness and concepts with which students may need extra practice.

How do you deal with kids who don't buy in or don't want to do the exit price?

The following steps are those that I follow to engage all my students:

1. Build a relationship of trust with the most challenging students on an individual basis. This can be done outside of the classroom, during lunch, between periods, after school, or over the phone. I also create an individualized contract that each student agrees to follow. Students help me craft these documents, and rewards and consequence are contingent upon their honoring the contracts. I assume responsibility for the success of all my students, and I will do whatever it takes to build a personal connection with each of them.

2. Ensure that all students truly understand the concept. I make sure each day's objective is simple and that it builds on what students already know. If an objective is too big, students easily get lost, get frustrated, and stop paying attention. Students should feel comfortable and regard the content as manageable and realistic. It is my responsibility as their teacher to make sure material is delivered in a way that is easy for them to understand. With this in mind, I ensure guided mastery through an interactive teach-back process, and I make an extra effort to reward kids with points toward their grade, occasional treats, or public recognition. If I explain the material so that

it seems easy to the target population, make them teach back the concept during class, and reward them for their effort, I can usually engage students to the point that they feel confident while tackling the exit price assignment.

3. Make students accountable for mastering the exit price. The incentive to show mastery on the exit price is that I grade the assignments during class. Most students care about their grades, and they will be more eager to buy in to the process if they perceive the exit price to be an "easy *A*." Consequences for not showing mastery include a poor grade (I will give them an *F* for the day) and a phone call to a coach, parent, or whomever I need to inform about the failing grade and lack of motivation. I also encourage students to come after school and finish the exit price. In short, I bother students so much that they won't want to fail the exit price.

If I am still unable to get the most challenging students to buy in, I start to think about damage control. As a last resort, I involve the school's attendance and behavior specialist or counselor and have him or her talk to the student. I won't allow a few disruptive students to remain in class and hurt the other students who do buy in and try hard. Although this happens rarely, I am sometimes forced to stop chasing those students in the interest of the other kids in class. No matter what I do, I can't win with every kid, but I can win with most kids.

How do you teach the essential material, especially if there is already a pacing guide that the district tells you to use?

These are the steps I use to create a timeline based on essential concepts:

1. Look at the mandatory state standards for the subject you teach. In my case, those are the content standards issued by the California Department of

Education for mathematics. I also look at released questions from the California Standards Tests; most states release sample questions from previous years' exams. With this as a framework, I determine which concepts—generally around 10 major concepts for the year—are the most essential for my students to master before they take the exam. Finally, I identify chapters and lessons in the textbook that teach and emphasize these essential concepts.

2. Make a rough timeline for the year based on your identified essential concepts. I reserve at least one month before the state exam to review released tests and test-taking strategies. During the course of the year, I might modify this timeline depending on the speed with which students master the essential concepts.

3. Defend your timeline with a well-reasoned rationale. If the principal or district administrators question me about why I have my own timeline, I tell them that I am using the district pacing guide, but I am simply emphasizing essential concepts listed in the state standards because I want my students to master those concepts. I never act as though I am completely discarding the district pacing guide. Rather, I am simply catering to my students' unique needs and teaching them according to their individual mastery levels. Finally, it is helpful to support this position with research by the National Center for Urban School Transformation that shows how the highest-performing urban schools in the country emphasize mastery of essential concepts over page-by-page coverage.

How do you grade for mastery during class when you have 30 kids at once?

1. Move around the room. I constantly circulate around the room and stop at every student's desk to glance at their work and assess that day's

concept. Obviously, I can't look at every problem for every student, so I spend more time with those students whom I know are already struggling (the target population).

2. Use peer tutoring to involve and motivate all students. I use superstar tutors whom I trust to do a good job, and they also circulate, check papers, and let me know how certain students are doing.

3. Collect all exit price papers at the end of the period. This demonstrates to students that I am serious about the assignment and want them to finish it. If I'm unable to glance at each paper, I'll skim through them during lunch or ask a teaching assistant to help me evaluate them. However, I usually grade all papers during class by efficiently circulating, looking at a few key problems, and focusing on the most struggling students.

CREATE Self-Evaluation Form

Instructional Aspect	How Do I Already Do This?	Suggestions for Improvement
Culturally Responsive Instruction		
Make standards-based content easy and relevant so students can understand.		
Explain concepts in a step-by-step manner and personally interact with each student.		
Rigorous Expectations and Rewards		
Create a positive learning environment in which it is easy to focus and learn.		
Clearly discuss and enforce your expectations with students.		
Develop relationships with the most challenging students and their parents.		
Enforce a system that personally rewards academic success and character development.		
Essentials-Focused Planning		
Emphasize essential skills in each day's objective, and spiral in previously taught material.		

CREATE Self-Evaluation Form (*continued*)

Instructional Aspect	How Do I Already Do This?	Suggestions for Improvement
Assessing for Mastery During Class		
Provide a measurable objective that can realistically be mastered in one class period.		
Make students teach back the material and demonstrate guided mastery during class.		
Establish and enforce a rigorous exit price that students must independently complete before they leave class.		
Reteach concepts based on results of teach-back activities and exit price grades.		
Test Models		
Regularly include model test questions on the exit price assignments.		
Extra One-on-One Tutoring for Struggling Students		
Provide additional one-on-one help to students who need it.		
If possible, use more advanced students to tutor struggling classmates.		

APPENDIX

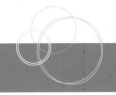
CULTURALLY RESPONSIVE RELATIONSHIPS

How can I develop a relationship with my students and learn about how they learn?

CULTURALLY RESPONSIVE CURRICULUM

Unit: _____

Essential Concepts/Standards	What strategies can I use to help students understand this concept?
•	•
•	•
•	•

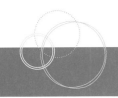

How can I actively engage all students, especially the target population, during my lessons?

RIGOROUS EXPECTATIONS FOR TEACHERS

My measurable goal for the year/semester is:

How will I use assessment data to evaluate my teaching effectiveness?

How will I differentiate instruction and raise student achievement?

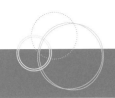
RIGOROUS EXPECTATIONS FOR STUDENTS

What year-long goal will my students strive to meet?

How will I help students internalize their goals?

How will I create a positive learning environment with few distractions?

REWARDING EXPECTATIONS

How will I create a class culture that rewards student learning?

How will I create a culture of positive feedback to motivate all students?

How will I reward student success, particularly among the target population?

How often will I reward student success?

Will rewards be attainable by a majority of the class?

Key Standards	Textbook Pages/Section	Prerequisite Skills/Teaching Notes	Released Test Questions	Timeline

Key Standards	Textbook Pages/Section	Prerequisite Skills/Teaching Notes	Released Test Questions	Timeline

TEACHER REFLECTION

ASSESS FOR MASTERY DURING CLASS

How will I scaffold instruction?

How will I ensure guided mastery during instruction?

How will I ensure guided mastery for the target population so they are ready for the exit price?

How will I ensure independent mastery?

How will I evaluate and grade exit price assignments to adequately reflect student learning?

How will I reteach/spiral missed concepts to ensure student mastery?

TEST MODELS

How will I frequently expose students to test models in the classroom?

How will I frequently expose students to test-taking strategies in the classroom?

How will I make sure students feel prepared and confident to succeed on standardized exams?

EXTRA ONE-ON-ONE TUTORING

How will I provide additional one-on-one tutoring for students?

How will I use other students to help struggling students?

How will I make sure that students who need help actually come for extra tutoring?

How will I use additional tutoring as a consequence for unacceptable behavior?

REFERENCES

Baltimore Curriculum Project. (n.d.). BCP History. Retrieved October 11, 2010, from http://www.baltimorecp.org/history.html

Benson, B. (1997, Nov.). Scaffolding. *English Journal, 86*(7), 126–127.

Bloom, B. (1984). The 2 sigma problem: The search for methods of group instruction as effective as one-to-one tutoring. *Educational Researcher, 13*(6), 4–16.

Bransford, J. D., Brown, A. L., & Cocking, R. R. (Eds.). (1999). *How people learn: Brain, mind, experience, and school.* Washington, DC: National Academy Press.

Brophy, J., & Good, T. (1986). Teacher behavior and student achievement. In M. C. Wittrock (Ed.), *Handbook of research on teaching,* 3rd ed. (pp. 328–375). New York: Macmillan.

Cobb, C. Jr., & Moses, R. (2001). *Radical Equations: Math literacy and civil rights.* Boston: Beacon Press.

Delpit, L. (1995). *Other people's children: Cultural conflict in the classroom.* New York: New Press.

Dewey, J. (1889/1976). *Middle works of John Dewey.* Carbondale, IL: Southern Illinois University Press. (Original work published 1889)

Education Trust. (2008). Achievement in California 2008: Fading gains, growing gaps. Retrieved from http://www.edtrust.org

Graesser, A. C., McNamara, D. S., & VanLehn, K. (2005). Scaffolding deep comprehension strategies through Point & Query, AutoTutor, and iSTART. *Educational Psychologist, 40,* 225–234.

Gutierrez, M. (2010, Aug. 29). Sacramento Teacher Inspires Math Turnaround at Grant High. Retrieved from http://www.sacbee.com/2010/08/29/2990212/sacramento-teacher-inspires-math.html

Hannel, I. (2009). Insufficient questioning. *Phi Delta Kappan, 91*(3), 65–69.

Hayles, V. R. (1991). African American strengths: A survey of empirical findings. In R. L. Jones (Ed.), *Black psychology* (3rd ed., pp. 379–400). Berkeley, CA: Cobb & Henry Publishers.

Johnson, J. F. (2009, Mar. 2). *What America should learn from high-performing urban schools.* Address presented at the National Association of Federal Education Program Administrators conference, Washington, DC. Retrieved from http://www.ncust.org

Kafele, B. K. (2009). *Motivating black males to achieve in school & in life.* Alexandria, VA: ASCD.

Kiewra, K. A. (2009). *Teaching how to learn: The teacher's guide to student success.* Thousand Oaks, CA: Corwin Press.

Kohn, A. (2000, Sept. 27) Standardized testing and its victims. Retrieved October 11, 2010, from http://www.alfiekohn.org/teaching/edweek/staiv.htm

Kuykendall, C. (1989). *Improving black student achievement by enhancing students' self image.* Chevy Chase, MD: The Mid-Atlantic Equity Center.

Ladson-Billings, G. (1994). *The dreamkeepers: Successful teachers of African American children.* San Francisco: Jossey-Bass.

League for Innovation in the Community College. (2006). *Getting Results: A professional development course for community college educators.* Available: http://www.league.org/gettingresults/web/index.html

Loveless, T. (2008). The *Misplaced math student: Lost in eighth-grade algebra. The 2008 Brown Center report on American education. Special release.* Washington, DC: Brookings Institution Press.

Marzano, R., Pickering, D., & Pollock, J. (2001). *Classroom instruction that works: Research-based strategies for increasing student achievement.* Alexandria, VA: ASCD.

McClure, L., Yonezawa, S., & Jones, M. (2010). Can school structures improve teacher student relationships? The relationship between advisory programs, personalization and students' academic achievement. *Education Policy Analysis Archives, 18*(17). Retrieved from http://epaa.asu.edu/ojs/article/view/719

National Center for Urban School Transformation. (2008). *What America should learn from high-performing urban schools.* Retrieved October 11, 2010, from www.ncust.org.

Noguera, P. (2003). *City schools and the American dream: Reclaiming the promise of public education.* New York: Teachers College Press.

Obama, B. H. (2004, July 27). Keynote address presented at the 2004 Democratic National Convention, Boston, MA. Retrieved from http://www.barackobama.com/2004/07/27/keynote_address_at_the_2004_de.php

Perry, S. (2009, Dec. 14). *Interview with Steve Perry on Anderson Cooper 360 Degrees/Interviewer: Anderson Cooper.* Retrieved October 11, 2010, from http://edition.cnn.com/TRANSCRIPTS/0912/14/acd.02.html

Perry, T. (2003). Up from the parched earth: Toward a theory of African American achievement. In T. Perry, C. Steele, & A. Hilliard (Eds.), *Young, gifted, and black: Promoting high achievement among African American students* (pp. 1–108). Boston: Beacon Press.

Poliakoff, M. B. (2002). Walking the walk of excellence: American Board certification for teachers. White House Conference on Preparing Tomorrow's Teachers. U.S. Department of Education. Retrieved from http://www2.ed.gov/admins/tchrqual/learn/preparingteachersconference/poliakoff.html

Popham, W. J. (2003). *Test better, teach better: The instructional role of assessment.* Alexandria, VA: ASCD.

Rohrbeck, C. A., Ginsburg-Block, M. D., Fantuzzo, J. W., & Miller, T. R. (2003). Peer-assisted learning interventions with elementary school students: A meta-analytic review. *Journal of Educational Psychology, 95*(2), 240–257.

Rosner, J. (2003, April 14). On white preferences. *The Nation,* 24. Available: http://www.jayrosner.com/publication-onwhitepreferences.html

Sanders, W. L., & Horn, S. P. (1994). The Tennessee value-added assessment system (TVAAS): Mixed-model methodology in educational assessment. *Journal of Personnel Evaluation in Education, 8*(3), 299–311.

Scruggs, T. E., & Mastropieri, M. A. (1992). *Teaching test-taking skills: Helping students show what they know.* Brookline, MA: Brookline Books.

Slavin, R. E. (1995). A model of effective instruction. *Educational Forum, 59*(2), 166–176.

Tauber, R. T. (1998). *Good or bad, what teachers expect from students they generally get!* Retrieved October 11, 2010, from http://www.eric.ed.gov/PDFS/ED426985.pdf

Tiberius, R., & Tipping, J. (1990). *Twelve principles of effective teaching and learning for which there is substantial empirical support.* Toronto: University of Toronto.

Weiss, B. D. (2007). *Health literacy and patient safety: Help patients understand: Manual for clinicians* (2nd ed.). Chicago: American Medical Association Foundation.

Wright, S. P., Horn, S. P., & Sanders, W. L. (1997). Teacher and classroom context effects on student achievement: Implications for teacher evaluation. *Journal of Personnel Evaluation in Education, 11*(1), 57–67.

Young, J. R. (2003, Oct. 10). Researchers charge racial bias on the SAT. *The Chronicle of Higher Education, 50*(7), A34–A35.

ABOUT THE AUTHOR

Dr. Kadhir "Raja" Rajagopal has been an educator since 2004. He is currently an algebra teacher at Grant Union High School, a low-income comprehensive urban high school in Sacramento, California. He is also an instructional coach for teachers in the Twin Rivers Unified School District and has taught in middle and high schools in East Oakland, California. Rajagopal was named a 2011 California Teacher of the Year.

Rajagopal completed his bachelor's degree at the University of California, Berkeley and earned his master's degree at the University of San Francisco. Recently, he completed his doctorate in education leadership, studying the impact of the CREATE model on student success in other teachers' classrooms. He and his students have presented the model at numerous statewide and national conferences, including the 2009 annual conference of the National Council of Teachers of Mathematics in Washington, D.C.

Rajagopal looks forward to sharing ideas and collaborating with other educators who are passionate about empowering marginalized populations to unlock their potential. He can be reached at kadhirr@yahoo.com or 510-333-1827.

Related ASCD Resources

At the time of publication, the following ASCD resources were available (ASCD stock numbers appear in parentheses). For up-to-date information about ASCD resources, go to www.ascd.org. You can search the complete archives of *Educational Leadership* at http://www.ascd.org/el.

ASCD Edge Group

Exchange ideas and connect with other educators interested in urban education on the social networking site ASCD Edge™ at http://ascdedge.ascd.org/

Print Products

Educating Oppositional and Defiant Children by Philip S. Hall and Nancy D. Hall (#103053)
Meeting Students Where They Live: Motivation in Urban Schools by Richard L. Curwin (#109110)
The Motivated Student: Unlocking the Enthusiasm for Learning by Bob Sullo (#109028)
Motivating Black Males to Achieve in School & in Life by Baruti K. Kafele (#109013)
Raising Black Students' Achievement Through Culturally Responsive Teaching by Johnnie McKinley (#110004)
Teaching English Language Learners Across the Content Areas by Judie Haynes and Debbie Zacarian (#109032)
Teaching with Poverty in Mind: What Being Poor Does to Kids' Brains and What Schools Can Do About It by Eric Jensen (#109074)
What Works in Schools: Translating Research into Action by Robert J. Marzano (#102271)

Videos

Educating English Language Learners: Connecting Language, Literacy, and Culture (#610012)
How to Involve All Parents in Your Diverse Community (#607056)
How to Use Students' Diverse Cultural Backgrounds to Enhance Academic Achievement (#608031DL)
Teaching with Poverty in Mind: Elementary and Secondary (#610135)

THE WHOLE CHILD The Whole Child Initiative helps schools and communities create learning environments that allow students to be healthy, safe, engaged, supported, and challenged. To learn more about other books and resources that relate to the whole child, visit www.wholechildeducation.org.

For more information: send e-mail to member@ascd.org; call 1-800-933-2723 or 703-578-9600, press 2; send a fax to 703-575-5400; or write to Information Services, ASCD, 1703 N. Beauregard St., Alexandria, VA 22311-1714 USA.